THE
P▮NLEADER
PATH

IDENTIFY, ENGAGE, AND DEVELOP
EFFECTIVE HUMAN AND AI LEADERSHIP
FOR YOUR ORGANIZATIONAL CULTURE

Reviews & Accolades

Dr. Gore brings unique insight on building strong, effective teams to everything she does. *The PinLeader Path* is no exception. Great leaders must develop their capacity for team-building, and this wisdom woven into the pages of this book will help shape the leaders of tomorrow.

MS. TRICIA CULLOP University of Miami Hurricanes Head Women's Basketball Coach

The PinLeader Path **is an informative and entertaining book** about effective leadership. The metaphor of a "PinLeader" is used to demonstrate new styles of leadership that are both engaging and collaborative, including the use of AI in organizational culture and leadership. The author uses examples of various styles of pins and fabrics to identify and develop creative ways in which today's leaders can respond to a variety of situations and issues; this book gives excellent examples of new ways to think about old problems. *The PinLeader Path* is a "must read" for a new generation of leaders.

DR. CYNTHIA BEEKLEY Retired Springfield Schools Superintendent

Dr. Shanda Gore brings more than 30 years in leadership to this book. In that time, I have witnessed her growth in the business and organizational world, which has positioned her to be where she is today. Dr. Gore's career path and education in leadership has helped her develop successful and winning PinLeader Path leadership strategies for every boardroom and business. As an entrepreneur, a seasoned higher education professional, and business consultant, she now shares her 25-plus years of corporate experience with her clients. Dr. Gore brings a wealth of advice and guidance to organizations looking for an edge in an ever-competitive marketplace. From Fortune 500 companies to high schools to colleges to those in the NFL and Big Ten, Dr. Gore has the solutions and strategies for the present and the future.

DR. DAVID STRUKEL Director, Burton D. Morgan Center for Integrated Entrepreneurship

Dr. Shanda Gore delivered an impactful and engaging presentation to our team! She focuses on the power of effective communication and the importance of finding common ground in building a positive company culture. Her insights were practical and inspiring, giving our team concrete tools to improve collaboration and create a more inclusive environment. The examples shared were relatable, and the session sparked thoughtful discussions that have already started influencing our daily interactions. We're grateful for the expertise and energy Dr. Gore brought to our team and look forward to seeing the long-term positive impact of her guidance.

MS. AMY L. FRIEDEL, EA, Owner, Padgett Business Services - Toledo

THE
PINLEADER
PATH

IDENTIFY, ENGAGE, AND DEVELOP
EFFECTIVE HUMAN AND AI LEADERSHIP
FOR YOUR ORGANIZATIONAL CULTURE

Dr. Shanda Gore

PinLeader Press
On-Point Books for Leaders
Sylvania, Ohio

The PinLeader Path Identify, Engage, and Develop Effective Human and AI Leadership for Your Organizational Culture

by Dr. Shanda Gore

PinLeader Press
On-Point Books for Leaders
Sylvania, Ohio

ISBN 978-1-965524-02-2 hardcover
ISBN 978-1-965524-00-8 paperback
ISBN 978-1-965524-01-5 e-book

Library of Congress Control Number: 2024920730

TABLE OF CONTENTS

INTRODUCTION: **The New Leadership Landscape**

Leadership has changed. Gone are the days when you could read a book or hear a catch phrase on leadership and trust that its wisdom is tried and true. The best leaders are not always those who work the hardest, put in the longest hours, show up early to get the worm, and stay late. In fact, today's top leaders are often those who work smarter with prioritized loads and who get straight to their goals with the help of talented teams that take on the work as a group. Those who stand at the forefront of the new leadership landscape are strong in mind, body, and spirit because they got good rest on their well-deserved vacations. They tend to their own needs and the needs of the teams they lead.

And that worm? Well, the sharpest leader in today's workforce is after greater sustainability and is far more interested in the seed than the worm. Smart leaders know the worm will come up from the soil eventually because the rain will bring it up. They know their reward is received in exchange for their consistent choice to nourish the environment that has been entrusted to them. As today's top executive leaders, HR managers, and change makers identify, engage, and develop the best human and artificial intelligence leaders for their leading-edge organizations, they set the ideal conditions for optimal performance from their teams, thereby accelerating and amplifying positive results for the organizations that employ them.

The Leadership Change Continuum

Leadership has changed and so have the notions around work. Some of the long-held perceptions and beliefs about leadership so heartily embraced by prior generations are still applicable in today's leadership landscape. Other statements, such as the adage that the most loyal employees will rise and eventually lead, are simply not true in today's leadership landscape. And what about work done by a non-human? How can today's organizations best incorporate and integrate artificial intelligence?

New concerns have emerged and modern leaders must address these concerns, yet the mandate for change and growth is continual and more pressing than ever in organizations of every shape and size. The sweeping change in leadership has its roots in how we manage our days *and* how our days manage us. Leaders can plan out as far as they would like, but factors outside their influence will always arise. Change is constant and behaviors, which flow from our reaction to that change, occur along a continuum. This is especially true for those who lead a team or an organization.

Consistency is often impossible because a particular work environment may not allow for consistency. What leaders can do and what they must do is to become self-aware. Be diligent with their approach. Be mindful of their skill set. Be in a mode of continual improvement. Effective leaders need to be aware of their triggers and recognize those triggers in others. The best leadership traits are obtainable, but leaders must first become intimately acquainted with what those traits are.

Solutions can still be found in leadership programs developed twenty years ago, but only those solutions that can be customized for the modern work environment will be effective long-term. Care, ethical starting points that incorporate a sense of fairness and justice, and a deep understanding of how to self-assess performance and effectively engage with the environment each play a role in effective leadership. And what happens when you throw in artificial intelligence (AI)? Can AI display care, be fair and just, and self-critique? These are some of the issues we will consider in the chapters that follow as together we explore how to navigate the ever-changing landscape of leadership.

A Crisis of Apathy

In our current climate we have a crisis of not caring. This is occurring not just within organizations but in society as a whole. Organizations are made up of individuals with their own lived experiences within society. It is not by chance that so many organizations are asking for trainings and workshops concerning civility and the ability to "place ourselves in someone else's shoes." What may have once seemed a given is now noted as a path of learning. We lean into others to determine what may be fair. Yet, in work environments around the globe, many no longer question themselves— largely because they fear that they might appear to be a failure. These individuals, often placed in positions of leadership, do not understand that failure is a necessary step toward improvement.

This apathy is a threat to much of how we interact with one another. How does such apathy show up in the workplace? It is often seen in an increasing lack of engagement, a decreasing interest in what is going on around us, and waning or lackluster passions that, if they were rekindled, might help motivate us to reach for innovative and effective solutions. Such apathy and the current crisis of not caring is costly to any organization.

Imagine coming into a workplace to discover papers strewn across the floor. No one has the desire to pick them up, so everyone just walks over the mess. This is a metaphor, however such a situation is commonplace in today's organizations and may well indicate that the skill to take appropriate action is not there. Or it may be a sign that those walking on top of those papers are mentally overwhelmed and do not take the time to care about the papers because their attention is focused on something else that they deem more important. Some may even claim it isn't really a big deal if they do or do not get their work done.

The lack of initiative to care for shared spaces is a symptom of a greater underlying issue. From misspellings and misaligned forecasts to the failure to provide basic follow up to customer inquiries, a lack of care and the lack of attention to detail is a sure indicator that customer service is the last priority for an organization. The revitalization of the work environments we share will be supported as organizations adopt more effective models for leadership and attract leaders who understand how to cultivate and shape the culture of the organization and lead their teams to care for the quality of their work and the work environment.

Now, more than ever, organizations need to be willing to discover new approaches and fresh perspectives on leadership. There is a need to step back and learn from a variety of voices from across the field in order to create a strong path forward. Never has it been so important to find innovative approaches that will spark passion and change in leaders. The costs associated with not doing so and remaining entrenched in apathy has never been greater, and organizations that do not find ways to address the accelerating pace of change and work with new technologies may well be in peril.

Within organizations, individual leaders are caught up in the crisis of apathy too. Many began with strong hearts and sharp minds, focused on driving toward results, but too quickly became mired in the mud of untended soil. Others become overwhelmed with the projects at hand and slowly began to engage less and less, slipping back from their role as leaders and into the role of managers. Often, they have failed to ask the most important questions of themselves and their teams.

What Successful Leaders Ask

The most successful leaders keep reaching, stretching, and learning. They are sharp, straight to the point, and strong. Not content to rest on their laurels, they are committed to a path of ongoing self growth and education. Nearly always, these leaders ask four key questions of themselves and of those they lead:

1. How can we sharpen ourselves?
2. How can we straighten up, avoid distractions, and stay on point?
3. How can we strengthen where we stand and move to where we want to be?
4. How might we go about planning in a manner that allows for change?

In the chapters that follow we will explore the PinLeader Path and investigate these questions in greater detail. First, let's look at a few of the broader themes that will give us greater insight into the leadership landscape. These themes set the stage for the ability to lead with greater effectiveness and confidence. The first of those themes is model thinking.

Model Thinking

A strong model provides successful leaders and the organizations, departments, teams, and projects they lead with a framework for success. Models provide structure. They provide leaders with a road map to check their own journeys against. Imagine knowing your destination but having no understanding about how to get to that destination. Perhaps you punch in an address in a GPS app only to find there are multiple options for routes that will enable you to eventually arrive at your destination.

Models allow for different options to reach a desired destination. Which model an organization selects is dependent upon the variables they have access to or choose to work with in any given situation. There could be a limited resources such as fuel, time, or even financial resources. Regardless of the model chosen, a leader must understand what resources she currently has at her disposal and what additional resources will be required.

There are, of course, many leadership models and approaches, the vast majority of which have something to teach us about how to lead. The key is to identify a model that is aligned with organizational goals, adaptable to new trends (i.e. the use of artificial intelligence in today's organizations), and appropriate to the context or environment. One model that stood out for me during a doctoral leadership development classes was Starratt's Multidimensional Ethic at Work in a School Setting model.[1] The model is centered around the power of introducing ethics into a school environment to support student learning. Starratt's research found that the schools that had the highest level of ethics were those rooted in care, justice, and critique.

Why consider ideal school environments or Starratt's model when our primary concern is the modern workplace? The reality is that every one of us is still in school: the school of everyday hard knocks and perpetual growth. The most successful leaders know and embrace this fact. They choose a path of lifelong learning and apply best approaches from a variety of sources.

PinLeader Considerations

Regardless of the environments we work in, we need to ask ourselves:

- What do our relationships ask of us?
- Who controls our relationships?
- What makes each of our relationships legitimate?
- What defines the nature of those relationships?
- Ultimately, how will we govern ourselves in the context of each of these relationships?

---

[1] Starratt, R. J. "Building an Ethical School: A Theory for Practice in Educational Leadership." *Educational Administration Quarterly*, 27, no. 2 (1991): 185-202.

PinPoint: For effective leadership within ethical organizations to take hold, reflection on these key questions is critical.

In any leadership role, relationships are at play and the quality of those relationships inform leadership success. These are questions you should ask yourself when you are faced with a roadblock. Return to these questions as you consider service that is both inward and outward facing and use them for ongoing self reflection.

The Importance of Caring

Never before have we been more connected through such a wide range of communication channels. However, we have also never been more prone to the dangers of care that comes too little or too late. This is due to the numbing effect of encountering the same roadblocks and issues over and over again without any meaningful resolution.

Relationships between people are becoming more challenged. With the onslaught of the global pandemic, even our personal space and the ability to reach out to others was challenged. We now have a generation that has grown up with fear of closeness embedded in their psyche. The expression of care, particularly in the workplace, has become a rarity, but the care we bring to our relationships is a vital component of our leadership capability. The best leaders bring their focus and attention to their relationships, including their relationship with themselves. Let's explore the various facets of how today's leaders can examine their relationships and make improvements to them, thereby amplifying their leadership capacity.

What Makes Life Meaningful

Critical thought and evaluation are a necessary and valuable tool for leaders who excel. Without such reflection, a leader's relationship with themselves and with others weakens. Begin by reflecting on what makes life meaningful and rewarding. Think of your quality of life. Has it increased or decreased in the last few years? Why is this? What do you see as the cause of any perceived change? If your quality of life is good or even excellent, have you considered how you might ensure your quality of life stays high regardless of changing circumstances?

Giving consideration to your quality of life communicates care not only for yourself but also for others around you. Your quality of life includes those connected to you both personally and professionally. Consider family members and friends, colleagues, bosses, partners, and team members. How might you contribute to a better quality of life for all?

Future Planning

All too often, individuals have a plan for their upcoming vacation, but they do not have a plan in place for wrapping up their professional lives or their business responsibilities. They may have a contingency plan for if it rains tomorrow but have no plan for what happens if the company they own or work within folds or closes its doors. Planning for the future is an essential action that demonstrates care for the future—your own future, the future of your family and friends, and the future for the organization you work for and the colleagues and associates who you work alongside day in and day out.

Developing Professionals

Investing in professional development without having to be prompted by external change is essential. Taking action not simply because you were told to do so but rather because you knew such action was necessary is a sign of self-care and self-respect. Also consider the personal and professional development needs of your staff and those you lead. Doing so demonstrates care. When leaders operate from a position of care, they raise the standard for others to do the same and naturally open new pathways to sustainable success.

 PinPoint: A goal is like a seed that has been planted. Taking action toward that goal is similar to watering the seed so it will grow. When well tended, your goals, like the seed, will bear the fruits of opportunity. Set a goal today to invest in yourself and in those you lead. Then, observe as these efforts yield a natural return for you and your team!

Culture Building

What about culture building? How does care tie into this aspect of leadership? The power of understanding that your customers and your employees are not all the same, and that you should not want them to be the same, is critical. It can make or break an organization. Those organizations that cater to only one group do so at their peril. Ignoring entire subgroups, whether internal or external to the organization, affects the bottom line and limits the opportunity for the organization to attract new audiences.

Perhaps you don't think you have the time to give consideration or attention to yet another audience. Perhaps it is easier to assume that a candidate may not be talented or smart enough to be on your team based on stereotypical perceptions or generalizations about the common characteristics of a cultural, racial, or ethnic group to which they belong. Such judgments are not only inaccurate in many cases, they also can bring diminishing returns for your organization. These assumptions may have a negative impact on your reputation, result in missed opportunities, and even decrease or entirely eliminate the potential for future sales.

Let me share an example that illustrates how costly a decision to overlook groups can be and how choosing to consider all groups will support your goals as a leader and benefit your organization. In the past, I have shifted investments away from organizations and persons who did not seem to care about my perspective. When I was treated in a way that, at best, assumed I could not manage money—an assumption based on stereotypes and not on reality, I moved my investments and engagements away from those companies. Worse for the organization in question, I shared my experience.

This organization lost further wealth holdings because others also began to move their funds. So where did I choose to go? I found an organization that took the time to understand my needs and values. The new firm was willing to meet with me and others to offer clear guidance and to provide a full picture of my investments. The new company demonstrated an ethic of care by embracing cultural enrichment and by honoring all customer groups without making sweeping assumptions about them.

Reaching Across Borders

What if your organization wants to do business overseas? How would you display care there? Care leads to trust which leads to relationships which leads to business. Conversely, a lack of care that comes in the form of ignoring customs or believing others will conform if you push your agenda is short-sighted. This can and will inevitably lead to undesirable results. Remember that to build relationships means also to know the value systems of those for whom you want to exhibit care.

Priorities and protocols for what is appropriate take dedicated research and study. The more prepared you are and the more research you do, the better the experience for everyone involved and the higher a likelihood of building trust for your company or organization with a variety of groups. Reaching across borders and around the world begins with being interested and demonstrating a willingness to learn.

Recognizing Potential

Care is demonstrated by taking the steps necessary to recognize hidden potential in current and prospective employees or team members and to take the added steps needed to nurture that potential. Such a course of action is a powerful retention tool. Coupled with empowering others to be part of creating or implementing a solution, this recognition of potential and an organization's choice to nurture that potential demonstrates a value for human dignity. When an organization consistently acts in accordance with that value, it builds trust in its employees and associates.

Successful leaders and the organizations they work for demonstrate care by evaluating progress. Evaluating progress comes in the form of scheduling regular and uninterrupted one-to-one meetings, allowing room for a mutually built agenda that includes professional development, and setting goals aligned with a clear career path for those involved. Setting benchmarks and clearly defining what constitutes success is an essential ingredient to the demonstration of care for those who work on behalf of the organization.

Being Accessible

Today respect, active listening, and inclusive behaviors are not a given across all organizations. In some circumstances, they may even be ignored or frowned upon. I recently attended a meeting at offices with stairs at the entrance and no accessibility for individuals in a wheelchair. When I asked those leading the meeting how they met with those who had walkers or were in wheelchairs, they stated no one had ever asked.

Now imagine if that individual had an accident, an unexpected surgery, or another situation that required him to be disabled. What answer would he give himself? What if his mobility was impacted long-term? Would he simply stop working? What if he could not afford to stop working but needed to go into an office? Accessibility provides human dignity and demonstrates care.

> **PinPoint:** Similar to the old saying "possession is 9/10ths of the law," in the workplace *perception* is 9/10ths of the law. Reality is only made clear through effective communication. If an organization hopes to create a welcoming environment for everyone, then it must create clear pathways that are accessible to all. This should be done *before* someone asks for it.

Wanting to be Present

Have you given consideration to the environment where you and your team perform the work you do? Another model that I appreciated and embraced during my doctoral journey was Alexander Astin's I-E-O (Inputs, Environments, Outcomes) model in his Student Involvement Theory, which underscores the idea that the environment plays a part in how care is viewed.[2]

Let's consider this model in light of a recent experience encountered in my consulting practice. A client requested help with improvements to his employee recruitment process. As I entered their company offices, I noticed that the lobby gave me the impression that I did not belong there. I did not see myself or anyone from a different race, ethnicity, or culture group in the images in that lobby. This left me with the impression that this organization did not want people like me there.

---

[2] Astin, A.W. "Student Involvement: A Developmental Theory for Higher Education." *Journal of College Student Development*, 40, no. 5 (1999): 518-529.

The interactionist theory of Vincent Tinto's Model of Institutional Departure explains how this "feeling" is exhibited in the college environment. One of the key ingredients of a welcoming environment on college and university campuses, Tinto asserts, is the presence of formal and informal social interactions.[3]

My initial impressions left me with the belief that I may not be fully welcomed to this organization. I discovered, however, that this conclusion was not accurate. In fact, it was far from the truth. When the organization's values and vision were clearly communicated, it became clear that it was the lack of care being communicated *through the environment* that was the issue, not the organization's commitment to connecting with diverse groups of individuals. I was able to make recommendations for the necessary changes, to include the physical environment, and the client was able to remedy the unwelcoming lobby and improve recruitment efforts.

Can Artificial Intelligence Care?

What are the considerations when it comes to nonhuman contact? Evolving by the moment, artificial intelligence (AI) provides a unique challenge. It is the new player on the scene for many organizations. When we view AI as a partner, building relationships rooted in a commitment to provide a trusted service to constituents, we may even believe that AI has the capacity to care. For example, when I asked Alexa if it cared about me, it replied "I think you are magnificent."

With current technology, I can schedule a particular affirmation or send a notification to remind loved ones that I love and care for them on a particular day. If I am asking for care, does that in any way decrease the value of a reply? It does not. When you tell others what you need, you are advocating for

---

[3] Tinto, Vincent. *Leaving College: Rethinking the Causes and Cures of Student Attrition*, 2nd Ed. (1993) Chicago: The University of Chicago Press.

yourself and for others. This is not unusual for humans. It is expected behavior. In a similar fashion, when AI serves as a means to solve a problem or lighten the work load, this too can be a clear and valued demonstration of care.

Justice for All

In order to better understand what is meant by justice, we can explore a myriad of different paths. Justice means many different things to many people. In the realm of leadership, justice can be understood as allowing others the opportunity for full engagement. Participation and active learning are key components that play a part in creating engagement in the workplace.

Unfortunately, justice gets a bad rap by those who may see it as a hindrance. Yet, anyone who has studied leadership would likely agree that successful organizations must include justice. No one wants to work for an organization where they are unjustly treated on a regular basis. Justice is an integral component of leadership and a signifier of an effective organization. Let's take a closer look at how the best leaders demonstrate a level of justice.

Having Your Presence Felt

How can one learn if one is not participating? Think about how just being present works in a business environment. There is an expectation that everyone who earns a salary will pull his or her weight on the team or within the organization. Someone in leadership allowing an employee or a group within the organization to show up at work but contribute nothing cheats the organization out of a valuable resource and signals injustice.

Any Chief Financial Officer (CFO) or company president would likely be disappointed in such a lack of leadership. Any human resource department would dread a report that included such findings. So much time and resources are invested into the recruitment and retention of good people. But what might stop an individual leader from participating fully in the environment? Sometimes bias and an unfair determination that the individual has nothing to contribute can put the brakes on full contribution.

What if someone was specifically uninvited or left off of a meeting request? Could it be because the meeting subject matter does not apply to the specific job duties of the team member? Could it be because those setting the meeting do not understand the duties and responsibilities of the uninvited team member, which led them to leave that individual off the attendee list? Or could it have been human error and simple oversight? All of this are possibilities.

Think of an instance when a meeting for all managers has been called to discuss a new policy that impacts workplace hours. What would happen if one of those managers was out on maternity leave? Do the leaders who called the meeting not hold the meeting because one manager is out on leave? No. Does the manager out on maternity leave get penalized for not being at the meeting? No. It becomes the responsibility of the leaders that are calling the meeting to consider that manager's inability to participate. Justice is demonstrated as those who are initiating the meeting work together to obtain the necessary policy changes to that leader's team. No manager should be retaliated against for taking the time that she is entitled to by the organization's own policies.

 PinPoint: Know the value of your time. Time is your most valuable commodity. Set an expectation that your time will be respected so you can feel good about your participation.

Now, think of an instance that may have occurred to you or around you where justice may have been overlooked, forgotten, or never considered in the first place. Balancing the rights of the team and their leaders with the needs of the organization is an important consideration, and the two can often seem to be at odds. Time is money and the goal of for-profit organizations is to maximize profits. For-profit organizations achieve this goal by getting the most value, which often translates as time, as they can from their employees. Philosophically we can debate that getting the most time from employees is not "right," but the reality is that maximizing productivity for profits is what a for-profit business is supposed to do.

Advocating for Your Presence

Once you understand you need to have access in order to fully participate and to allow others to see the full scope of your value, you will find the motivation to advocate for your access. Anything within an organization that squashes, reduces, or minimizes the talent or value of individuals or groups steals time from the organization. I have witnessed firsthand a number of scenarios brought to my firm's attention where individuals felt "left out" and ignored. Comments such as "What are they paying me for?" or "I feel unseen and unheard" are commonplace in such dysfunctional organizations.

The larger the organization, the more frequently such a situation occurs. The actual mode of operation in such organizations is in direct opposition to the reason they have these individuals on their payroll. It is poor leadership that intentionally leaves talent on the table, and it is the responsibility of that organization to ensure that this is not happening. This responsibility rests on the shoulders of the organization's executive leadership. An organization's top leaders must become vigilant in seeking out input and information about access for all groups across the organization. Leaders must keep a careful watch on issues that may be buried in a pile of complaints.

Justice, Time, and Nonprofits

Now let's consider nonprofits. Everything mentioned previously also applies to not-for-profit organizations. There is still a need to maximize time, but in nonprofit organizations there is a common good, for-a-cause mission at play. Depending on how you feel (note that I am referring to an emotional consideration here), this use of time may be a great one. If you value your time and the cause, you have a win-win.

Justice is served here just as it is for a for-profit organization. You have the right to make a choice about where you want to work and spend your time. That may seem obvious, but there have been instances where both the organization's leadership and those on teams within those organizations forget they are employed "at will," excluding a bargaining or union contract. When considering work in a for-profit organization or a not-for-profit organization, take the time to become familiar with expectations such as financial compensation and the opportunity for flex schedules.

Allocating Resources

A final way of thinking about justice in the environment is to consider the allocation of organizational resources. With all parts being equal, you may think this will be easy to determine. Again, not so fast. The question comes down to who determines what is fair in terms of allocation. Can a human being with flaws and biases determine who should get what and when they should receive it? Are such decisions deemed more credible when decided by committee vote or democratic decision-making?

Consider a situation where the leader could not make a decision or did not have a policy to fall back on and, as such, left the decision up to a vote. How many people thought that was fair? Depending on the resource, debates may start and be ongoing in such situations. It is not only about the resource. It is also about the credibility of the leader.

What if the leader is deemed to be unfair? What if the leader is the one who seems to secure all the resources? Perhaps a vote is considered a better option by the group. Such a course of action may even be suggested based upon perceptions within the organization. It is possible in such situations that AI can provide a justice call. The major caveat is that leaders must be mindful that AI is only as good as the way in which it has been programmed. When it comes to resource allocation, biases based on limited input or partial information will play a significant role in how AI is able to respond to inquiries or contribute to fair and just decisions.

Assessing Ourselves

What is the value of questioning why we do what we do? Why is it important to know and understand the hierarchies in which we work? Critique, beginning with self-critique, provides powerful information that can enhance both the quality of our relationships and our ability to lead effectively. Questioning ourselves is a skill that each of us must master. Not everyone can do it. Not everyone *wants* to do it. Self-critique can be difficult and requires ongoing practice.

When it comes to critique, we must apply it to ourselves, to teams across the organization, and to even organizational philosophies. Knowing where we fall in hierarchies and understanding our own privilege and power within an organization requires solid self awareness and consistent self-inquiry. Despite what some may want you to believe, leaders are not born with their skill set intact. Leaders develop over time. The belief that individuals are born with any skill or knowledge, thereby making them more appropriate for a role above another group, can be considered elitist. Tread carefully when this philosophy has been or is being adopted and promoted.

Self-Assessing What?

Where are you right now with your resources? Is your workplace tight on funds? Do you feel guilty when you witness another department struggle for resources while you plan your department's next trip? You may view having resources and talking about those resources with others that do not have access to them as having a negative connotation or think of it as an undesirable quality.

Perhaps you consider it a privilege that has been earned but also see this as a topic of conversation to be avoided because somebody may feel bad. If so, consider a situation where every employee or participant in an organization had clear knowledge of the full scope of their power and also had insight into added areas of influence that they may be missing. How would this affect your organization's ability to lead the field? In most cases, it would significantly boost capacity and expand effectiveness.

Effective leaders must develop the maturity and self-confidence to handle criticism, even if and when it does not feel constructive. Leaders must hone the skill of discernment. Although many leaders believe they are engaged in self-critique and discernment, deep self reflection takes a significant investment of time and focus. It is a skill that requires continual refinement.

 PinPoint: The ability to become a constructive critic of yourself is a place of growth.

Imagine a time when you were called into a meeting with a leader who pointed out the seven things you did incorrectly in a past meeting. What would you do in such a situation? Would you argue? Would you wait, take notes, and thank them for the feedback? What if the critique contained a grain of truth? What if the leader's perception was different from your own assessment?

The best course of action is often to remain calm and thank the leader for providing guidance and feedback. If you believe you are right and he is wrong, it is important to remember both the benefits and costs of correcting him before you speak. You can point out what you believe to be true, especially if you feel the perception of your competency is at question, but there's truly no need to argue. Keep it simple. The simplest path is often the best path.

Using Power Wisely

When was the last time you sat down and asked yourself who you were influencing? Who on your team is impacted by your decisions and direction? It is easy to say we are fair and nonjudgemental, but we are human and all humans have biases. In trainings, I had an individual walk up to me to explain that he did not have any biases. He insisted he was not impacted by external forces and knew that the decisions he made provided fair and equal treatment.

Did I think this was accurate? No. In fact, I was even more worried for him because everyone has biases and being in denial of those biases creates more problems. We must each be responsible for our own biases. The first task is to become aware of what those biases are and to consider how our biases impact those in our circle of influence. Then we must do the hard work to overcome our tendency to discount the impact of those biases. Finally, we must take action to surmount the unconscious bias brought to our awareness. But should you be totally reliant on yourself to do this work? Let's turn our attention to the topic of support as it pertains to truthful assessment. How can we have constructive conversations in the workplace?

Constructive Conversations

One of the best ways a leader can ensure they are being thorough in evaluating bias and motive is to surround themselves with individuals who provide a solid thread of healthy critique. If your leadership skills need attention and the way you manage is tied to your brand, then treat yourself like you would treat your own company. Get a personal board of directors. From *Forbes* to *Harvard Business Review* to academic leadership classes, a resounding number of recommendations suggest leaders need strong connections to others who can provide critique and guidance.

Each seat at the table can represent aspects and expressions that are important to you. Career, personal life, spiritual, financial, and business are just a few of the options. Selecting an individual who can provide helpful feedback, rather than constant positive affirmations, is a good starting point. An example of a less than ideal choice would be to place a parent as a member of your personal board of directors. This may create a bias toward positivity and affirmation without an appropriate level of critique. Perhaps there are plenty of parents who handed out healthy critiques but these were likely tempered by praise and comments of affirmation.

When it comes to praise and affirmation, it is important to note that this same bias also applies to artificial intelligence. AI does not appear to be critical enough currently to fulfill the role of unbiased advisor as it is currently in a "set to please" mode. Likewise, someone close to you or reporting to you might provide poor advice from a position of benign intent. It is your responsibility to determine who can fulfill the role of advisor as objectively as possible.

 PinPoint: A solid and carefully selected Personal Board of Directors helps with evaluating oneself.

Clearing the Path

Now that we have explored caring, justice, and self assessment, let's consider how these ideals interface with the three components of a PinLeader Path —sharpness, the ability to get straight to the point, and strength. We will delve into each of these key aspects of the successful PinLeader in the foundational chapters of this book. Here at the outset it is important to establish that these characteristics do not exist in a vacuum. Rather, they are inextricably interwoven with the winning approach of today's best leaders.

Here are the three qualities of leaders on the PinLeader Path:

1. The Sharp Leader

The *sharpness* of a leader, which is made evident through education and experience, comes through self-awareness coupled with justice. Education teaches us to be more observant and to listen. We develop the ability to allow ourselves to be graded or evaluated based on our performance. Justice comes with experience. It requires a knowledge of what is morally right and wrong. Ultimately, justice leads us back to care.

2. The Straight to the Point Leader

Straightforward thinking and aligned action that, with appropriate planning, leads *straight* to desired outcomes are connected with care for one's self, one's team, and the organization as a whole. This trait is shared by the best leaders. It is closely associated with an attitude of care and operating with fairness and justice. It also requires the ability to think critically and to adjust as needed based on how you evaluate yourself and how others are evaluating you.

3. The Strong Leader

Strength of character requires care and empathy. Contrary to popular belief, loyalty and moral standards are not passé. In fact, they are needed more than ever. When coupled with respect, a leader's strength of character instills a greater degree of confidence in those who are led by that leader. Strong leaders also have a greater capacity for justice and fairness.

The most effective leaders are sharp, straight to the point, and strong. It is the interplay of these qualities that combine to create the most powerful of leaders—the PinLeader. Let's get into that pin and talk more about what, specifically, creates the kind of leader who has staying power, the leader who is fully equipped to lead today's organizations forward with fortitude and finesse.

CHAPTER 1: **The PinLeader Path**

There's nothing like having a roadmap to success—a distinct path that represents an effective approach to your everyday practice and incorporates the qualities of your character. Those with clear direction outwardly show confidence. They are memorable. When it comes to personal success, there is a formula that can be replicated. When a leader follows a clear and distinct path, it leads to an approach that leaves a mark on those around the leader, a positive force that others admire and want to emulate.

Now, think about how you are leaving a mark on your organization. What are others saying about your leadership? Does it measure up to the expectations of the organization? Even more importantly, does it rise to the level of your own standards? Perhaps you think you have your own style of doing things and there's no more room for improvement because you have already obtained degrees, certifications, and key accomplishments that have led to accolades in your field.

Certainly there are great leaders doing great work and you may fall into that category, but the best leaders exhibit shared characteristics. They follow a proven formula that works. The best leaders never rest on their laurels. They are always changing, evolving, and sharpening their points. Without a commitment to continual growth and improvement there are only dull, stagnant approaches. Those who default to such practices are not forward thinkers. Strong leaders have a plan but pivot when needed. They weather the worst conditions because they are prepared.

Leaders fill a need. They serve others, and their service is needed. The path to becoming an effective leader takes both time and effort. Successful leaders follow patterns, sometimes consciously and other times unconsciously, that have solid foundations. They are rooted in a path that has led them to where they are.

Just as a sewing project needs pins to hold the pieces of fabric together to prepare for sewing with needle and thread, organizations need strong leaders placed in key positions to pull plans and projects together. Like that pin, the effective leader must be placed strategically to ensure the fabric holds.

There are so many theories about leadership. The study of leadership affords us the opportunity to learn about the top habits of the most effective leaders, discover what those leaders do to ensure their success, and discern how that success can be replicated. Armed with the knowledge that clear patterns will emerge and make a difference, those who will lead the next generation of exceptional organizations have an opportunity to connect these dots. Furthermore, they have an obligation to themselves and to those who depend upon them to know and discover the best paths to follow and the best approaches to adopt.

Leaders certainly have unique styles, but the top echelon of leaders share common traits. Let's take a closer look at the three most important qualities, which are three areas of mastery along the PinLeader Path.

The PinLeader™ Path

The best leaders focus on three key principles that intersect and also proportionately impact one another. These include: *Strength*, *Sharpness*, and *Straightforwardness*. The goal for leaders is to recognize and connect to the power of each one of these elements within themselves and within their organizations. Understanding the various leadership profiles when recruiting for teams or when planning for succession helps organizations to develop models and know what traits to look for when identifying, engaging, and developing potential leaders.

For those who are not sure where they currently fit, the PinLeader Path and the leadership profiles we will discuss can provide a clear roadmap and key characteristics to embrace. Let's start by pinning down definitions.

Pinning Down Definitions

The most effective leaders are sharp. They exhibit experience and education in their respective areas. They demonstrate strength of character by utilizing the basic rules of integrity, honesty, and transparency. In this way, they earn the trust of their constituents or teams. They follow a strategic plan and are straightforward, yet they know when to pivot. For the sake of our discussion of the overall PinLeader Path, let's start with an overview of those three principles and establish clear definitions:

- *Sharpness* is defined as the level of education and experience in a desired area or industry.

- *Strength* is defined as the level of ability to take on challenges and to keep the fabric of an organization together by strong character and will.

- *Straightforwardness* is defined as the ability to set a path, typically by developing an effective strategic plan that clearly outlines where you are going, while also maintaining the ability to pivot.

Understanding and being fully aware of where you are on the continuum of leadership effectiveness is important, especially when designing a strategic planning for your organization. During interviews I have conducted with leaders across different industries, it has become clear that nearly all effective leaders have undergone a level of professional development that has included self examination.

This commitment to self-awareness and self-growth has often provided these leaders with greater clarity on the approach they prefer to use when interacting with team members. Knowing where you are and where you want to be is the first step to becoming a more effective leader. There is a myriad of ways to look at your own behaviors and to obtain feedback from others in order to determine where you fall on the leadership continuum. The remainder of this book will introduce you to best practices. Let's explore the PinLeader Path.

Creating the PinLeader Path

It all started with the humble sewing pin. In May of 2006, I first introduced the PinLeader model as a pathway to effective leadership to a group of doctoral students who led organizations in both the private and public sectors. Using the analogy of a simple sewing pin to describe full connection to essential leadership qualities, this model introduced the integral steps one must take to become an effective leader.

Originally intended as a way of explaining the power of a high functioning team led by an effective manager who adopted PinLeader characteristics, the PinLeader Path quickly evolved from these initial thoughts. As a leadership coach, I began to apply the PinLeader concept with staff and clients that included several requests for additional presentations.

Further discussions took place around the relevance of the PinLeader Path in multiple settings, from traditional businesses and nonprofit organizations to health care, education, and finance and then stretching into athletics and sustainability-focused arenas. As requests for information and training grew, the need to document the PinLeader Path became more urgent. Nearly twenty years later, with new tools such as AI having arrived on the scene, this leadership approach has been applied successfully in both for-profit and nonprofit organizations. It is time to bring the PinLeader Path to the world.

The PinLeader Path is clear but flexible. It can be easily adapted across industries. Having used this system for two decades, with updates to include new concepts and tools, I have shared the PinLeader Path in workshops and successfully applied it in my own consulting practice. I am now prepared to share with confidence what the effective PinLeader Path looks like and what it does not.

There are, of course, a number of theories and models that incorporate the word "pin" into their titles. How is the PinLeader Path distinct? The PinLeader Path stands apart as it addresses human leaders and also acknowledges and includes artificial intelligence. This differentiator is key as we are living in a time when AI is quickly becoming a primary contributor.

This book will assist with your own self-awareness. It will help you identify desirable and sometimes challenging PinLeader attributes and provide suggested responses in situations when the wrong leadership approach arises. It will support you in reaching for the lofty goal of a sustainable and effective culture that can survive and thrive with or without you.

Let the *pinning* begin!

The Making of a Sewing Pin

For such a tiny tool, the sewing pin can vary widely in its composition and also in its uses. Depending on the job, one may need a specific kind of pin. That's right, there is more than one pin for the job; but if you want to sew well, choose your pin wisely!

According to the *Just to Sew* website, what determines the best sewing pin is the project at hand.[4] So what does a pin do? The sewing pin holds fabric pieces in place and allows patterns to be utilized to help guide the project.

A sewing pin is rated based on how good it is at accomplishing these things. Among those factors that are taken into consideration when ranking pin performance are what each pin is made of, or its composition, and how that pin holds up when put to the test, or its durability. Special attention is given to whether the pin is heat resistant, for example.

Other factors considered when evaluating a pin's performance include: the number of pins available for a particular project, the type of project a pin is best suited for, the length of the pin (given the understanding that the type of fabric dictates the specific pin size needed), and how pins are packaged and shipped. All of these variables impact the ability of the pin to do its job.

 PinPoint: PinLeaders who come from the most challenging circumstances within other organizations are some of the most valuable employees.

Can That Pin Take the Heat?

Similar to a type of sewing pin that is made of metal, a leader on the PinLeader Path often has an inherent strength that makes that leader heat-resistant. The leader who can hang on when times are tough is the most desirable leader to have at the helm in today's organizations. Purposefully driven and with a sincere desire to see their organization through the sizzle of a hot iron which often comes in the form of internal change, economic

---

[4] "10 Best Sewing Pins Sets Reviewed in Detail," accessed April 7, 2024, https://justtosew.org/best-sewing-pins.

downturns, or an unexpected upheaval, the strong leader understands the phrase "this too shall pass" and lives by it.

The PinLeader who can keep calm and hold steady will not melt under the pressure of such heat. In this sense, the PinLeader is much like what is commonly called a Color Scissor sewing pin. The Color Scissor pin has the highest ratings[5], thanks to its unique features such as its glass head and metal shaft. That glass head does not melt under the heat of an iron in the way a pin with a plastic head would. Instead, the Color Scissor pin contains a steel shaft and is solid and durable, able to sustain its form despite high temperature and pressure.

But if the most desirable pins are heat resistant, why aren't they all made that way? It is all about the job, what budgets allow for, where the organization wants to go, and how fast it wants to get there. As in any situation, costs do play a factor and the most valuable pins always cost more based on their highly desirable attributes, their resistance to heat being one of the most important characteristics.

Investing in the Pin

The old saying that you get what you pay for is at play here. Paying more for the best leader for your organization is not only wise; it is also necessary if the organization is to survive and thrive. If the person in a hiring position expects to be patted on the back for making lowball offers to talent, think again. The act of cutting corners and not offering what a leader is worth is actually costing your organization. Paying more in order to obtain a higher quality pin (a PinLeader) for your organization also means there is a greater likelihood that the new hire will hold the fabric of

[5] "10 Best Sewing Pins Sets Reviewed in Detail," accessed April 7, 2024, https://justtosew.org/best-sewing-pins.

the organization together better. The best leaders are those who are appropriately compensated and supported with a full staff and robust resources. They know the organizational plan and goals and have helped create some, if not all, of those plans.

After COVID, several highly talented PinLeaders left the employee workforce either due to burn out, worry, health-related reasons or as a result of downsizing on the part of the organization. They may have decided not to work within existing organizations and instead created their own organizations, immersing themselves wholeheartedly in the start-up revolution of the early 2020s. So who is left and where does that leave the organization? AI is one virtual employee that will never leave the organization and not to be overlooked. But who will replace those human leaders who do choose to move on?

PinPoint: AI is one virtual assistant that will never leave the organization. Make sure to sign in and keep conversations going whatever platform you choose to utilize, so it learns continuously and can therefore provide the best guidance possible for you and your organization.

Recruiting Top Talent

The first thing to remember is that the perception that someone is following a PinLeader Path is exactly what it is—a perception. Organizations may replace highly effective leaders with less proven leaders based on what they think those individuals can do for the organizations. In many cases, funds previously earmarked for a compensation package intended to attract an excellent leader are dispersed, and new leaders are recommended solely on word of mouth and not on a proven track record.

Any organization should have a goal to invest in the best talent and not allow salary considerations to be the only driving point with how they secure talent. Lazy approaches to not checking references and relying on popularity will get that organization, at best, a new leader who may not be strong enough to take the heat. Another circumstance that may occur is that a newly recruited leader may be placed in a role without the proper tools and resources. For example, appropriate training and a review of the soft skills are the tools needed to make the necessary connections.

If the organization simply decides that budgets are just not at a level to afford an effective leader, then a plan should be put in place to reprioritize budgets in order to attract the right person for the role. One bad pin can become the undoing of an entire organization. But what if you need more than one great leader? Do organizations require more than one highly effective leader to hold the fabric together?

Does More Mean Better?

In nearly any project the more pins that are used the better the fabric of the project holds together. However, there is a threshold of no return. Every pattern provides direction to where pins can be placed, often providing the precise number of pins needed to secure the fabric. The head count for the necessary number of PinLeaders within an organization works in a similar fashion. The number and kind of goals and corresponding actions in a strategic plan will dictate the number of PinLeaders needed within the organizational structure.

Those leaders on the PinLeader Path do need colleagues and other effective leaders who have the education and experience to handle other departments, areas, or sections within the fabric of the organization. The strength of any organization rests on its leadership. When a great leader is an influencer or at the helm, other leaders will follow suit and be attracted to the organization. The highest caliber leaders attract one another.

PinPoint: Create regular opportunities for leaders across the organization to interact and share ideas with one another.

Multiple Pins for the Win

A key benefit of more than one great leader within an organization is the expansion of the number of projects, goals, or organizational challenges that can be addressed at any given time. Consistency in approach with a solid line of communication between leaders creates continuity for the organization and a culture of working together.

Employees who are watching leaders who are on the PinLeader Path rise to ever higher levels of achievement and success want to be part of that success. I have never met anyone who went to work stating that they wanted to work on a failing team. In my experience, no employee wants their leaders to fail them or the organization. In fact, effective leaders who decide to leave the organization often take other leaders with them and their employees also sometimes follow them. In addition, PinLeaders naturally create opportunities for other PinLeaders to rise up and take on key responsibilities that help hold the fabric together.

Length Is a Necessary Consideration

How long can a leader remain effective in his or her position? How long does any leader need to be in the organization for it to be profitable, organized, and effective? At what point does the ability to meet or exceed goals and stay on purpose begin to wane? With everything, it just depends on the job.

Within your organization, you may have a number of PinLeaders who can sustain the heat of challenges, but every organization must determine how long is too long for a leader to stay in one position or leadership role.

Let's assume your organization has looked at the budget and hired the best leader available, one who is like that heat resistant pin. Even so, there are heat resistant pins who are not placed in positions that empower them to hold larger projects together.

For example, in sewing, pins with extra-fine glass heads may be used. These pins are super sharp and strong but are not meant to hold multiple layers together. Likewise, some leaders within the organization may be meant to serve in a role that is limited in scope or temporary in duration. Brevity has its place and need. Consider, for example, the leader who has all three attributes of a PinLeader: sharpness, strength of character, and a straightforward approach to planning. Some leaders are meant to be in their roles for longer than others.

PinPoint: If your organization is in a budget crunch and unable to attract strong PinLeaders, work with the CFO to review budgets for professional development to help create opportunities for those with strong leadership potential.

While some leaders are meant to stay for the long haul, others are put in place to execute a three-year or five-year plans. Still others are tasked with a sole focus of getting the organization back on track. There is a clear understanding that they will not have an extended stay or a longer time invested in the organization. Does that make that leader less than desirable? Not at all.

In fact, depending upon the circumstances, there may even be an understanding that the leader serve as an interim employee, completing the leadership task and only then assisting with onboarding a successor. What about the successor's team? Those on the PinLeader Path who served in an interim position may also assist the successor, who may remain in place for a longer period of time, with team selection. In some cases, the

PinLeader who served in a short-term capacity within the organization may become a strong consultant to the organization.

In my own tenure, I have served as an executive coach for both large and small organizations. The majority of leaders I work with are placed in organizations for the long term. However, sometimes there are leaders who want to transition out due to retirement plans or other opportunities on the horizon that will allow them to move in a different direction. These shorter pins are often equally as sharp as those in place for the long haul. They have assessed what they want for themselves and carefully considered the manner in which they want to leave their present organizations.

Either way, a great organization with a strong fabric or culture should recognize their PinLeaders needs and desires and readily assist them with that transition. This can be achieved by hiring a coach, mentor, or other qualified support that may be external to the organization's human resources (HR) department, particularly if HR does not have a specified talent development area or have an exit plan identified in advance. Being a short PinLeader requires strategic thinking and a good grasp of an appropriate exit plan. This is a common area of weakness in many organizations.

Good PinLeaders recognize the short-term plan and their own needs. Great PinLeaders recognize the multiple layers of organizational plans as well as their own needs and put both short- and long-term plans in place for themselves and their teams. The best leaders also have a deep understanding of the organization's short-term and long-term planning requirements and ensure teams are in place to form and implement strategy at the appropriate junctures.

The Function of HR

Human resource team members are a vital piece of the organization's fabric. The mark of an effective HR leader is that leader's ability to guide teams. The best HR leaders can also conduct strong exit interviews, taking the data collected from those exit interviews and incorporating it into a solid departmental strategic plan that supports employee retention and recruitment. Strong HR leaders know the organization's goal and make key recommendations. They have the capacity to advise without the fear of reprisal. Ultimately strong leaders do not work autonomously but are independent enough to step back and make non-influenced decisions that benefit the organization and its employees.

> **PinPoint:** Budget for HR personnel to obtain professional development. If you do not have an HR professional, seek an external qualified consultant who can assist with leadership development within your organization.

The function of HR is not to be a watchdog but rather to be a companion to PinLeaders who need solid data and support to recruit and retain great talent. PinLeaders may become "short pins" when their tenure is based solely on whether they are supported by a fully responsive HR department. Whether leaders can develop a reciprocal relationship with this key component to the fabric of the institution will be a determining factor in their success.

This reciprocal relationship is demonstrated by transparent, consistent effective communications that include listening on both the leadership and HR personnel. Not achieving this reciprocal relationship goes beyond losing great talent and not being able to recruit effective employees; it has real and significant financial implications. In 2017, it was reported that it takes one fifth of that employee's salary to get him or her replaced, not including all the downtime required to bring someone new up to speed and also not accounting for the loss of institutional memory.[6]

Imagine if that good employee is on a path to become a great leader? What if that employee was well respected by other valuable employees who then decided to follow the leader out the door or leave on their own when encouraged by those they see as mentors to do so? What a tremendous and costly loss to the organization in terms of time and talent.

On the contrary, there are HR professionals who do not follow up, are power driven, and should have been replaced once they lost their ability to be strong leaders themselves. These individuals are typically short lived, as are the poor leaders who selected them. The fear of negative publicity or backlash within the organization drives these individuals to ask others to handle those pieces they know are not aligned with good management practices or sound policy. This scenario amounts to one weak pin using another weak pin in the hopes that no one will notice the bad behavior and less than stellar results.

Transparency and Communication

Fortunately, employees often do notice and talk amongst themselves, sometimes seeking outside help to remedy the situation. Are there attempts to silence those employees who do speak up? Sometimes the organization is concerned that a choice to seek outside help or counsel which may lead to a perception that they are not responsive to the needs of employees. The best course of action here is to encourage more discussions within the organization. It is imperative that employees feel that they can find a safe place to talk about anything that may be confusing, challenging, or may create additional anxiety.

----

[6] "Why Do Employees Stay? A Clear Career Path and Good Pay, for Starters," https://hbr.org/2017/03/why-do-employees-stay-a-clear-career-path-and-good-pay-for-starters 4/7/2024.

Remember that if employees do not have the information that will calm their fears, then there is a greater possibility that some employees will "make up" facts to fill the void. Think of an instance when a rumor started based on only a small bit of information. The rumor may have had some element of truth to it, even if it was only a small tidbit. It is not until the organization confirms or denies that information that it should become a topic of discussion.

PinPoint: Rumors are used as truth when facts are not shared. This can work against an organization's culture. Effective communication builds positive culture.

Building a Culture of Trust

The HR professionals who are struggling to balance what management wants with compliance requirements and their own moral beliefs must be able to develop courage and learn to live with the actions and decisions made. Witnessing a change in leadership that appears unethical or one which conflicts with an HR department that is attempting to advise based on another standard will often spell disaster.

Once employees feel that they cannot trust the HR department to do anything about what they perceive to be an injustice, it is most likely that leaders and their teams in other areas of the organization will seek outside counsel. Soon other departments will follow their lead. Leaders on the PinLeader Path understand this and do all they can to work with employees and not bury any issues that have truth attached to them.

PinPoint: Leaders who practice repeated avoidance lose credibility. Using a "bulldog" to carry out actions that may be perceived as "mean" or engaging in "bad cop" behaviors and attempt to drive an individual out of an organization will cost the organization good employees. Also, there is a higher likelihood of poor public relations, a challenge to recruiting good employees, and potentially a criminal charge or a court case. Don't do it.

The Color of the Pin

The best leaders, like the highly rated Color Scissor pin, are pliable. They can hold all types of challenging projects together and can successfully secure the pattern to the fabric in order to finish a project successfully. They can embrace an array of fabric types.

Color is noted as a desirable attribute by many who sew, but does the color of the pin affect its function? Does it matter what that pin looks like? No. The head of the Color Scissor pin can be any number of colors. The color of the pin does not matter if the other attributes are the same. It is only important that you select the right pin for the job.

If you do not have the right pin in place, that pin cannot be effective to do the role that you need it to do. However, those who sew often reach for the next pin with little thought given to whether the pink pins are better than the blue ones. Does the color matter if all the pins have the same ability to hold a project together? What qualifies the pin? Some may say it depends on what the project requires.

However, there are benefits to be achieved by diversifying the color of pins in the mix of pins you choose for a particular task or project. The different colors help make it easier to see the different parts of the pattern and can break up the monotony that would result from the same color pin appearing repeatedly. Should the color of PinLeaders matter in the workplace? While the answer is no, diversity within the mix of PinLeaders can help bring a much needed variation of thought and experience in order to get the job done at the highest levels of achievement.

Think of a time you may have led or been part of a team meeting where each member was asked to come up with a suggestion for how to solve a problem. Did each team member come up with the same suggestion? Most likely each contributing individual did not. The team member may have tapped into his own past experiences, education, and a variety of information that may be unique to him. Without the variety of thought, experience, and education that comes from a diversified team, there would have been less contribution. The best solution may have potentially been lost.

Traditionalists, whether in terms of sewing pins or PinLeaders, may demand that you use whatever pin is available—even if the pins or PinLeaders available represent only a single uniform color. Others may decide that they prefer the color of the pins to be different as this helps them better see where to sew and adds more variety to the project. All types of colors are available but ultimately all pins, and all PinLeaders, perform the same job.

Let's ask ourselves some basic questions here:

- Can you say you do not see the color of the pin head?

- Would you say that it is important that the pins that have unique colors and are inherently different from the rest of the pins?

- Is it necessary to have a certain number or percentage of color pins?

Questions for PinLeaders selecting a team:

- Does the color of the person matter in terms of their ability to meet the challenge and create solutions?
- On the other hand, can you truly say you do not see the color of the person on the team?
- Do you need all members of the team to look the same and be the same color in order to ensure the best outcome?

If you said the color does not matter but have found yourself ever claiming that you "don't see color," you are in a challenging position and may not even know it. Consider this: What if there is truly no "color" to choose from because one member of your team is now Artificial Intelligence?

 PinPoint: Statements made to team members which may ignore physical or other obvious differences or attributes can be offensive. These statements are called a micro invalidation and can create resentment and an unwelcoming environment.

The reality is that, unless you are blind or color blind, you *will* see color in working with humans. We all have biases—both positives and negative—with regard to our perceptions and in terms of how we select our "pins" and enlist for particular roles and responsibilities. An unconscious bias may be present. In other words, you may have the expectation that a particular pin or leader at a certain level in the organization will be a certain type or color. If you limit what color pin can be used in a particular role based solely on color, you may miss out on the best leaders for the job.

A myriad of questions arises when we consider color, which in the case of leaders might also include ethnic heritage, culture, and origin story. One increasingly important consideration comes with the acknowledgement that AI is now an integral member of the team in nearly every organization. What if you do not trust the leader because it is not human? There is also the matter of self-examination and a consideration of what "colors" you bring to the table and how your unique background makes you different.

How do you view yourself? Does the color of your skin or your unique heritage intersect with your ability to do your job? What we contribute is often the sum total of our experiences, education, culture, and environment. These factors make each individual unique and contribute to the ability for each individual to bring innovative solutions based on their individual perceptions of the problem that is presented.

You may have heard the phrase "Variety is the spice of life." This is also true of a good organizational culture. Anyone downplaying variety does not understand the power of doing business to attract customers, clients, or donors. Gone are the days of a single story, product, or standard as being adopted, bought, or supported. That occurs only in finite circumstances. Companies who have figured out that their audience members may well have differing needs and want variety in the options presented to them, not only in terms of product but also in terms of who they may be working alongside, will find their customers returning to do business with them.

There is more than one reason why companies appreciate their Employee Resource Groups (ERG)s or affinity groups. They can tap these groups for sales efforts and call upon them to create new market opportunities. The color of the leader does not matter in competency, but it does matter if a leader can bring a fresh perspective that will help the organization better penetrate into new market areas.

Assessing a PinLeader

Let's explore how we can determine if that new perspective can truly positively impact the organization. Although individual leaders in your organization may have completed various assessments or evaluations, these are not always a clear indicator of whether leaders are currently functioning in an optimal way or is effective in their role. Assessments should be considered as a way to help leaders become more self aware, but they should not be relied upon as the only tool to determine if employees are ready to lead within the organization.

The Clifton StrengthsFinder® and the Myers-Briggs® assessments are two of the most common assessments used by organizations to determine the characteristics of top leaders. There are, however, other assessments that should be incorporated alongside these two standbys. Some of the alternative assessments can be more telling in terms of how leaders may interact and make decisions. They can be even more powerful in determining why leaders did what they did. These alternative assessments have to do with biases which can be both negative and positive toward a concept, organization, or individual(s). PinLeaders become stronger once they are more aware of such biases.

 PinPoint: Every individual has biases. Anyone stating that they do not have a bias is less self aware and will benefit from further professional development.

To Bias or Not to Bias

There are a number of bias tests out there, to include free options such as the Implicit Association Test (IAT) in the Project Implicit study conducted by Harvard University.[7] There are also tests that require an investment, such as the Intercultural Development Inventory (IDI) which is an assessment that supports building cultural competence.[8] Within a growing number of tests and assessments to determine bias, it is important to realize that there are those biases that are outwardly known or explicit and those unconsciously present or implicit.

Most of the mentioned testing involves implicit bias, but what if a leader is openly admitting their bias? This is explicit bias and it makes it easier to quickly determine if such bias will potentially harm the organization or individual. Most employees understand their leaders' biases when that bias is repeated by the leader.

Consider a statement such as, "We will be changing a process because we need to prepare for the future." Not everyone will agree with the change or move wholeheartedly toward it. However, if the leader is clear on why the change is needed and how it will benefit not only the organization but the employee, the change will be adopted and more individuals within the organization will become positively biased toward change.

Now, bias toward those who are considered "like minded" is not unusual and should not be considered a "bad" thing. This is considered "ingroup" bias versus those that you may not trust which would be "outgroup" bias. A bias is considered negative when it is acted upon in such a way that brings harm or diminishes something or someone.

_____

[7] Implicit, Accessed May 11, 2024, https://implicit.harvard.edu/implicit/takeatest.html

[8] The Intercultural Development Inventory (IDI), Accessed May 11, 2024, https://www.idiinventory.com

Assessing Out of a Job

Susan's first duty as the new leader of the human resource department was to handle the performance review process for the company. She was excited to engage in this important work and set up timelines for completion. She was asked to obtain a full 100 percent compliance, with evaluations to be turned in.

Susan knew her predecessors had attempted to get the managers to do this with each of their employees but had failed to collect all the reviews for the employee files. She reviewed all processes, policies and set up new deadlines. She then met with senior leaders to ensure they were in agreement with her new procedures, which included a self assessment to be completed by each employee and provided to their managers. The managers would then conduct their evaluations based upon these assessments.

Based on feedback from emails, senior leadership was glad to have her guidance and new processes in place. Susan shared the process with her HR team so that they could answer questions of anyone who needed help with the evaluation. A month before the performance reviews were due from the departments, Susan began to hear about difficulties with the forms.

Managers were struggling with filling out the online form. They did not understand the ordinal, 1-5 rating scale (1 is poor, 2 is unsatisfactory, 3 is satisfactory, 4 is very satisfactory, 5 is outstanding) and were concerned that their employees did not understand the form in such a way that would allow them to accurately assess themselves. In some instances, team members came to HR with long written examples and explanations of their work to achieve their point. In other instances, team members did not know how to write up their "proof" of the work that had been accomplished.

By the time the due date arrived, Susan determined she only had 35 percent of reviews turned in, and many of these reviews had ratings of 5 (the highest possible) across all categories. Susan decided to issue an email stating she was rejecting the evaluations that had been turned in, because she believed the ratings were "impossible" for team members to have achieved. She told managers to downgrade their teams and advise them to be "more realistic" in their assessments.

Within two weeks of issuing the email, Susan was called into a meeting with senior leaders and told to back off of her demands and "fix" the score sheets. Susan decided that her HR team was "incompetent" with communicating how to utilize the form and set another deadline for completion, blaming the high scoring on self-rater bias. Managers noted that Susan was being "aggressive" in handling the reviews and rejected her new deadline demands. Susan began to fire department personnel and, during her three years of managing the department, she never reached even a 50 percent evaluation completion rate. She was dismissed for poor performance.

PINLEADER INTERACTIVE

Join the PinLeader Path Community! Scan the QR code below to access the PinLeader Interactive. Use the following questions for further discussion and consideration.

The Case of Assessing Out of a Job

- What do you think Susan did right? What did she do wrong?

- What improvements in this process would you make? Why?

- Is 100 percent compliance with evaluation possible? Why or why not?

- Have you experienced self-rater bias? How was it managed?

- What professional development opportunities would you recommend to Susan in this situation?

CHAPTER 2: **PinLeader Sharp**

This financial opportunity was special. The stakes were high, and Tanya knew that if she could secure this grant, it would mean a significant boost in revenue. That could help underwrite a number of new jobs focused in an area closely aligned with the organization's mission. As an administrator, she had been contacted about the opportunity but she needed a project lead.

Tanya was not sure who in the organization she should recruit for this project. No matter what, Tanya knew she needed someone with the credentials to win the opportunity. Several potential leads on her list had multiple academic degrees. If she did not make her decision soon, she was worried that the opportunity would go to another organization.

As she started to vet the possibilities, she came down to two potential candidates. Both met baseline requirements in terms of their educational backgrounds. However, she made her final decision on one vital difference: one of the two candidates had hands-on experience working with the population that would be served with the grant. With a strong leader, an understanding of a good mission fit, and collaborators who stepped forward to support the grant and who respected the leader she had chosen, Tanya secured the sizable grant for her organization.

Tanya's ability to sharpen her discernment and enroll the person who was the best match for the opportunity was a true asset to her organization. By stepping back to reassess what leadership education and experience would best serve the immediate goal of securing the grant and the long-term goal of a successful, well-run project, she advanced the organization's ability to fulfill its mission. Her astute observation and careful evaluation of project needs, along with her consideration of both short-term and long-term organizational objectives and a willingness to look deeper and beyond the credentials listed on paper led to a positive outcome.

In this example, Tanya exhibited the first PinLeader Path quality of sharpness, setting up the project for optimal performance and success. She was advised to prioritize experience over education but both were needed. Her ability to make this difficult hiring choice demonstrated leadership qualities and garnered respect.

Tanya used her own experience and education and followed the PinLeader Path to demonstrate her ability to identify talent and secure financial resources. The respect and credibility she gained put her on the fast track to promotion and resulted in further invitations to participate in decision-making meetings.

PinLeader Considerations

- If Tanya had been told to prioritize education over experience, what type of outcome would she have gotten?
- How can you determine the right balance between experience and education when evaluating new team members?
- How did Tanya's own sharpness play into her success?

How Sharp Are You?

Sharp leaders acknowledge both their strengths and their weaknesses, and interactions with sharp leaders on the PinLeader Path reveal a pattern of strong self-reflection. Sometimes leaders even seek outside assistance with that reflection. How sharp are you when facing difficult choices? Think back to the last time you took time to think about how you may be impacting your team.

As a leader, do you build in times for self-evaluation? Honest reflection is required if a leader is to rise to the level of excellence. How well do you know your own biases? How frequently do you step back and examine what assumptions might be informing the choices you make?

A leader's decisions are often tied to that individual's particular biases. No one is going to be perfect or eliminate all bias. The definition of perfection is in the eye of the beholder, and the eye of the beholder is not objective. The important lesson for leaders is to know and understand their own biases and to ensure their leadership decisions do not create further division and harm.

> **PinPoint:** Bias exists in every organization and within every leader. Those who know their biases and choose to do no harm based on those biases are strong leaders on the PinLeader Path.

Education and Experience

Let us come to a common ground of understanding about what constitutes this first PinLeader quality of being sharp. The definition we have presented for "sharpness" includes a leader's education coupled with his experience. This is often the first set of criteria used to determine who should be placed in a job or role, but looking at past education and experience alone is not enough to ensure a good match.

Sharpness demands an ongoing process of self education. In other words, those given responsibility for recruitment and hiring need to assess if a candidate has the willingness to be a life-long learner.

Questions for the Hiring Manager to Consider

- Does this candidate have the desire for professional development?
- Does this candidate have the skill and acumen to look at both the micro and the macro level?
- Does this candidate have the confidence to be a leader?

- Does this candidate incorporate succession planning into his or her leadership philosophy?

In our current climate, a "good education" has become synonymous with attending a college or university that requires a higher financial investment or is known as a top-tier school. Typically, greater value is placed on more exclusive educational opportunities. This reality requires attention by those leaders who want to distinguish themselves from others seeking the best positions. Candidates who are seeking to reach the next leadership level and those who would like to take on expanded opportunities within their current organizations set themselves apart by giving consideration to professional development.

Questions for a Leadership Candidate to Consider

- Have I updated my credentials?
- Have I put myself through rigorous professional development in the last year
- Have I kept track of the many ways I have vested in the growth and development of myself and my team?

The Value of Education

As an individual with a doctoral degree, I can attest that my education has assisted me in guiding others. It has given me keen observation skills and the ability to discern when others are not educated in a particular arena or subject area. Education is important, but a lack of the "perfect education" should not be used as a crutch or a reason to limit your leadership. Sayings such as "fake it 'til you make it" and labels like "the imposter syndrome" are often used as a way to avoid or circumvent the hard work required to create sharpness and can plant doubts in your own self-perception. These statements may even lead you to conclude that you do not deserve to be recognized as a leader in whatever space you occupy.

In the modern world of work, there is no doubt that those with the most education are the candidates who are most sought after. Yet, there are ways to augment your education. When reading a nonfiction book on a particular topic, for example, professionals can tap into experts who have invested time in research in order to bring forward the facts. If a person is demonstrating and teaching statistics, you would expect her to have gone to school and to have done well in those subject areas. The sharp PinLeader values education and never stops learning.

 PinPoint: Seek out leaders who have education and demonstrated experience in their areas. Expertise "creep" happens when professionals claim to have experience in an area they have never actually worked in before.

The Value of Experience

Like education, experience is an indicator of sharpness. The more years of demonstrated experience an individual has in an area, the more likely that individual can lead others toward viable solutions and help the team anticipate potential pitfalls. However, make no mistake that education without experience or experience without education can be disastrous.

Imagine the first time a new firefighter enters a burning building. With enough practice and sound training and education about what to do, the firefighter will be confident. The more experience that individual has the more likely others will follow that firefighter's lead. We tend to listen to and place our trust in those who have the attributes of both education and experience. One without the other is not enough.

Now, some would recommend a mentor to help that firefighter along with preparation. However, has anyone ever stopped a firefighter from entering a burning building to ask him how many years of education or experience he possesses? Does anyone stop him to ask who his mentor is? This is highly unlikely.

We simply assume that the firefighter must know what he is doing. He must have done this before. He must have acquired some level of education that gave him the skills needed to run the equipment and make quick and effective decisions. All of these factors lead to a level of trust that is not usually second guessed. The past experiences of that firefighter have further strengthened his value to the department and, most importantly, to the people whose lives and homes may one day depend upon the skill and expertise developed through years of service.

Trust the Process, Trust the Equipment

Trust is earned, and it is by choosing the right processes and the right tools that a leader gets where he or she needs to go. Let's stay with the firefighter example. As a wife of a retired firefighter with 29 years of experience within his department, I have learned about the value of trusting the process and trusting your equipment. My husband's mantra to "trust the equipment" is what gave him the confidence to climb up the ladders and to take the hose into a building on fire.

He trusted that the ladder would hold him. He trusted that the hose would channel the water and allow him to direct its flow. Without the right tools, neither he or any other firefighter could be successful. He trusted his department to prepare him adequately and, over time, he developed the skill and confidence to mentor and lead others when called to do so. Likewise, whatever industry or type of organization a leader is in, when that leader trusts the process and trusts the equipment, he or she sets themselves up to naturally develop a sharpness that will enhance their leadership capabilities. There is an added benefit of time savings involved here as well.

Great leaders have the confidence to make gutsy calls. They know that when they make a decision, they don't have to retrace or second guess their decision because they have done their due diligence to make the right decision. This circle of confidence is created first by sharpening skills with the right tools and being prepared to use those tools. The best leaders then move forward with an inherent trust in their teams and the process. The "point" of such PinLeaders is sharp and they stand ready to penetrate into the fabric when the call to lead through change comes.

How Dullness Impacts the PinLeader Path

Sharpness is a reflection of skill mastery and achievement largely based on time. Time spent in deepening your education and in broadening your experience can be considered time well spent. You may know and hold in high regard individuals who have years of experience and education in their respected areas. Consider how this education and experience builds trust and creates sharpness on the job and in life.

Where there is a lack of consistency in a leader's experience or the currency of his education, there is a need for caution. That caution means that that pin is or has become dull. When leaders have not honed their skills or have allowed those skills to become tarnished by time or underuse, they lose their sharpness—and their edge in the competitive leadership landscape.

The lack of knowing the trends, being stuck in a time warp based on old concepts or how things "used to be" are some of the symptoms of such a condition. To be clear, this has nothing to do with physical age or the tenure of a leader. Rather, loss of sharpness or the condition of "dullness" most often can be linked to apathy. When a professional does not reach for the best sources of information and stay on top of what is needed for the organization and his own personal growth, that professional sacrifices sharpness, the first and arguably most essential PinLeader differentiator.

Have you ever met a leader who is highly educated and has years of experience but is vastly behind the times with philosophy, business practice, or language usage? Perhaps this leader throws together phrases to make it sound as if he has done the work. Such a person may pretend to possess the proper education and be current with the demands of a leader serving within the current environment.

Disappointment sets in when you find this person, who you thought was a good leader and who may have at one point been sharp, is actually rather dull in his capacity to lead and to manage the complex situations for which you thought they were prepared. They may be older or younger in terms of age, but age does not play a significant role in terms of leadership capability. Rather, relevant experience, education, and expertise are three determining factors in a leader's ability to excel in a chosen field or environment.

If you have allowed your skills to get rusty or if you are out of date with current philosophy and practice, it is not too late to begin again. There have been leaders who have stated that they specifically surround themselves with new talent to discover fresh perspectives and find new solutions to existing challenges. They state that it is refreshing, and they have chosen to bring these individuals to meetings so that others can be exposed to them.

But those leaders do not usually arrive at that determination on their own. Sometimes it takes those around a leader to point out the need for new, fresh ideas. For others, it starts with a simple and straightforward honest assessment.

Think of your own leadership. Where do you need to stretch? What skills could you master that would exponentially improve your ability to lead your team? What experience is missing from your portfolio? Make a list and make a plan to level up your education and experience. Then put in the time it takes to be sharp again.

 PinPoint: Dull pins have the ability to be sharp again, if they put in the time and effort required.

Teamwork and Turning Things Around

To be clear, being PinLeader sharp has nothing to do with titles. There are plenty of presidents, vice presidents, and other senior level administrators who do not know what they are doing. Nor do they have the critical experience needed to manage a crisis, let alone lead others out of crisis. They were, sometimes admittedly, dull in areas they needed to be sharp in and repeatedly demonstrated this through a number of noticeable missteps.

Now, everyone makes mistakes, but it is critical that individuals learn from those mistakes. The savvy leaders move quickly to identify mentors who can assist them in bolstering their areas of weakness—not to save them or other team members for whom they are ultimately responsible, but rather to help them course correct and set a clear course forward along the PinLeader Path.

 PinPoint: In leadership, there are no knights in shining armor. It takes a team to work together to bring an organization back in line. Course correction starts with strong and clearly defined goals.

Let me emphasize the point very clearly. Team members who look a leader in the eye and state "You are here to save us" have not taken responsibility for their own part in saving themselves. Leadership is not about saving the organization. Instead, leadership is a pathway to building effective teams that are led by sharp leaders who can guide that team through decision-making processes to get to a solution that may or may not have consensus built into it.

Leadership—especially sharp, on-point leadership—can be a lonely road. Not knowing this at the outset will present a significant challenge to those who do not know the full story about what has occurred to get the organization into the situation it is facing.

Self-Reflection and Growth

To keep sharp and prevent an inevitable dulling, a leader must employ a process of constant self reflection. The effective leader hones the ability to listen to others and seeks out guidance from others. She engages in both personal or professional development in order to remain sharp. Once a leader discovers that she cannot keep up with her level of expertise, it is time to seek a new area to begin to build up your education and experience.

Notice I did not suggest leaving everything on the table or abandoning ship. To be an effective leader you will always need to check to see if your sharpness is sufficient to lead the team through tough times or navigate the challenges of a fabric or culture you did not anticipate or expect.

Returning to our core analogy of the pin and leadership, what if a pin is used all the time? Overuse creates dullness. Being worn out and overworked has an impact on your ability to get sharp and stay sharp. Rest and renewal are required. Strong leaders set boundaries and understand the need to take care of themselves so that they can effectively care for their teams and the projects for which they are responsible. When leaders prioritize their own needs for growth and self-reflection, sharpness is the result.

Getting Sharp

The ability to lead a team and influence that team is only achieved by experience. Those on the PinLeader Path know the strengths and weaknesses of their team. They move quickly when they see interpersonal challenges cropping up among team members and make the necessary changes. Is there ever hesitation? Yes, as there should be. Any leader who rushes toward change without a full investigation of the impact is not utilizing the best of their intelligences. In some roles, quick thinking is necessary, but a knee-jerk reaction can have devastating consequences. Sharp leaders balance the desire for a quick fix with careful consideration of the overall dynamics at play.

Take the case of a leader asked to recruit as many individuals into the organization as possible within a six-month time frame. The leader moved quickly and brought on all the team members to ensure success and met the goal. However, there was one problem. When the droves of new team members showed up, the organization was not able to handle the influx.

The leader who did the work was successful but the effort ultimately failed because no one paused to consider the big picture or to ensure the organization could absorb the high numbers of new employees that would be required. The leader failed to have the right people in the right seats up front in order to recognize this problem.

To appropriately support the large number of incoming employees, the leader in this organization needed to guide the departments and strengthen their supports to reach their different goals. Within two years, half of the new recruits were gone. The organization was reeling from a missed budget forecast that had counted on those individuals as contributing to the bottom line. All the time and effort originally invested in those individuals was also lost.

Poor timing? Not at all.

Poor planning and a lack of experience?

Absolutely.

 PinPoint: Being proactive is always best but not always possible. Effective leaders are rarely caught off guard because they stay sharp and consider the possible outcomes of different scenarios.

Overrated and Underprepared

In the noted recruitment scenario, it did not matter what the education level of the new recruits was. In this case, there were highly-trained physicians and certified decision makers, but that still did not save the organization from the costly misstep. Had proper experience been added into the recruitment mix by those leading the initiative, it would have become apparent that such a drastic change would put stressors on the organization.

Had those with the proper education and experience been a part of the implementation team, someone might have asked the right questions and tempered the decision to bring as many new people as possible into the organization to achieve the business goal. Having the experience *and* education that contributes to this vital understanding lies at the heart of being sharp.

Let's get to the point of being overrated. Think of a time when someone new was brought in to the organization and placed in a leadership position. He may have come highly recommended by a board member because he was a strong influencer in the community. We all know of instances when a candidate looked great on paper or key organizational contributors or influencers were good friends with him, yet these leaders did not deliver.

Any leader tasked with the selection of a new team member or even an outside consultant should not rely solely on influencers. Sometimes there are hidden agendas there and you have to uncover them in order to reveal the reason for the referral. If a new recruit was overrated, time will reveal that truth. Lack of education or experience will show regardless of how nice or friendly the person is. Hiring done solely on the candidate's ability to make people feel good does not mean that individual is sharp enough to handle the project or manage the team.

Let's take a look at another instance of this, which comes when friends recommend friends without truly understanding the individual's skillset is another pitfall. These kinds of decisions may also demonstrate a level of favoritism that cannot be ignored. Getting to the point means evaluating key measures, such as a proven ability to meet deadlines and consistently deliver results. Fact checking will spell success for any leader adding to their team or relying on others to help them do so. It is vital to develop the ability to discern which candidates may be overrated or underprepared for the task at hand.

Staying Sharp

Are you at the top of your game? Have you achieved the most education you can in your area of expertise? What about your experience? When was the last time you sought out a professional development opportunity or signed on for a new challenge? The key for any leader is to continue to seek out learning opportunities. By staying on top of trends, you increase your ability to lead a team successfully. Perceived credibility and trust are not to be expected. They are always earned. By periodically assessing and then seeking a way of fine tuning your skills, you will earn the trust of your team, your peers, and your organization's leadership.

Skills sharpen with practice, and practice makes for real experience. Stay sharp by implementing a plan for honing your leadership abilities and putting them into practice in your day-to-day experience.

 PinPoint: You become a more credible leader when you lead by example, foster environments of fact finding, and encourage questions. Inquiring minds are the strongest minds in problem solving!

Credibility and Credentials

When it comes to achieving credibility there are a few factors that influence how a leader is perceived, and those factors work in conjunction with one another. Respect and trust are coupled together, and the degree of trust and respect earned is determined not only by demonstration of your leadership capability but also by other's perceptions of your credibility. External influences may play a factor in promoting greater credibility, and those factors may have nothing to do with a leader's education and experience.

Think of a time when a leader was placed in a position of power but did not possess the credentials typically thought necessary in order to do the job. Many may have questioned how that individual got the position. Through time, however, this leader may have demonstrated the ability to fulfill her role through demonstrated success and decisive actions. Conversely, you may have heard the leader hired was favored above a more qualified candidate because she was perceived as more "likeable" or a "better fit" for the organization. Perhaps the hiring manager knew this particular individual was not going to make any changes without first asking permission and viewed this as a positive.

The credibility gained by a leader can also be characterized as an External Reinforced Affirmation or ERA. The greater the ERA, the higher the respect and trust the leader will garner. The more negative the ERA, the more difficult it will be for the leader to hold on to respect and trust. At the top is the leader that can continuously demonstrate with actions that support the ERA that she has been given. Once those actions and demonstrations dwindle, so does the level of trust and respect. This is visually represented in *Figure 1: The PinLeader Respect & Trust Zone.*

FIGURE 1: THE PINLEADER RESPECT & TRUST ZONE

What if the leader has gained all the knowledge, skills, and experiences without any demonstration of desired actions and outcomes? When is enough is enough? Where does the organization draw the line? There comes a point when a leader invests too much time acquiring greater experience and education and is no longer actively leading the team to the degree necessary for optimal progress. This is the equivalent of a sharp pin sitting in its comfortable pin cushion just waiting to be used.

Conversely, some leaders may be all too eager to dive in and prove their ability; however, the right project, team, or fabric is needed in order for a leader to excel. Once the level of sharpness is determined through their education and experience, it is important for leaders to consider the specific area of intelligence where they can excel. There is not just one level of intelligence for leaders to consider. Let's look at the four distinct types of intelligence that are directly tied to the sharpness of the PinLeader.

The Four Intelligences

There are researchers who suggest that there are multiple intelligences and others who argue that there is one, more general baseline intelligence.[9] Those leaders who motivate and influence their teams in the most effective manner often rely on each one of the four intelligences below and combine them to their advantage. These four intelligences allow leaders to tackle common roadblocks, challenges, and delays and move projects forward with greater ease and effectiveness.

The four types of intelligence every leader needs to employ are:

- emotional intelligence,
- intrapersonal intelligence,
- interpersonal intelligence, and
- (due to the rapid rise in the use of technology) artificial intelligence.

---

[9] Morgan, H. (2021). Howard Gardner's "Multiple Intelligences Theory and his Ideas on Promoting Creativity." F. Reisman (Ed.), *Celebrating Giants and Trailblazers: A-Z of Who's Who in Creativity Research and Related Fields*: pp.124-141. London, UK: KIE Publications.

Emotional Intelligence

Keep your emotions in check. Think before you react. Avoid showing fear, anxiety, or anger in front of the team or other leaders. Does any of this advice sound familiar? Consider whether living up to any of these common recommendations is even possible. Or desirable. When is too much or too little a good and when is it a bad thing? This is the better question to ask. Still, there's no question that the ability to accurately read and respond to workplace situations is a skill that nearly all adept leaders possess.

Emotional intelligence is the ability to use emotions to communicate a message effectively with others. One clear indicator of individuals who have emotional intelligence is their ability to perceive, evaluate, and relate well to others. Think of the times in the workplace when voices were raised and emotions ran high over a decision made out of the team's control. The leaders who were calm and level headed may have been seen as the most credible individuals by some but at the same time may have been perceived as uncaring by others.

It should be stressed that such perceptions are totally in the eye of the beholder. Knowing that there is someone with a level head in a time of crisis is a good thing. However, demonstrating a lack of empathy or not expressing concern during the crisis is not a positive trait.

A true leader must understand where his own emotional intelligence falls, not based on a simple "good" or "bad" value judgment but based on where he falls along the continuum. Each person will have unique triggers. The key for sharp leaders is to recognize that they may have a reaction that is not always aligned with what may be the most effective or prudent course of action.

Self-awareness is a top priority for a leader, and it is equally important to bring that awareness to the teams a leader manages and directs.

Remember that others may hold a different perspective and have triggers that are distinct from your own. Perhaps, for example, a personal or family matter has influenced a reaction by a team member who does not demonstrate a strong degree of emotional intelligence.

The best part of being sharp in terms of emotional intelligence is that it provides you and others a level of grace in terms of making mistakes. Think of a time when you wished someone would have said or reacted differently or when perhaps your reaction to another person was not ideal. A true leader understands these swings happen. She is proactive and works to ensure a safe environment that allows for the expression of appropriate emotion while also protecting others from the brunt of an unwarranted outburst. By demonstrating an understanding of emotional intelligence, those on the PinLeader Path gain credibility and are perceived as being sharp in a way that goes beyond the expected.

Intrapersonal Intelligence

Know thy self. Engage in daydreams to envision what's possible. Know the difference in reality and fantasy. These actions and activities are commonplace for those individuals with strong intrapersonal intelligence. Intrapersonal intelligence builds on the first intelligence, emotional intelligence, but is also distinct from it. Intrapersonal intelligence allows for the creative mind to flourish as it creates new pathways for innovative solutions and future progress.

Leaders with high intrapersonal intelligence reflect each day. They frequently check in with their dreams, hopes, and vision for themselves before attempting to communicate their message to others. They explore new ideas and, in many respects, "find themselves" before they act. They have the high level of emotional intelligence needed to understand what passions drive them but take those noted motivations a step further by recognizing what they may or may not need to do to achieve their goals.

PinLeaders who exhibit high levels of intrapersonal intelligence also know their own strengths and weaknesses. They are strong enough to admit when they are weak in particular area. By continuing to reflect on a daily basis, they leverage their strengths and seek external resources to sharpen the areas they have identified for improvement.

 PinPoint: Executive coaching for those in their first few years of leadership assists leaders be sharper and stronger in each of the four intelligences.

Another attribute that contributes to intrapersonal intelligence is a choice to be a life-long learner. This is often demonstrated by a leader who seeks out helpful certifications and furthers his education without being prompted. It is not unusual to find leaders taking courses, hiring an executive coach, or learning from multiple resources that offer differing perspectives and viewpoints.

Keeping a journal or diary to reflect on their leadership journey, to include both challenges and positive situations, is another action leaders with strong intrapersonal intelligence often take. In their journals, leaders who possess skill in this intelligence may note how they arrived at a solution with a particular challenge area.

To achieve the best results with intrapersonal intelligence, a leader must make the practice of self-reflection a daily habit. Strong leaders find this to be a critical part of their day. In fact, many make it their first priority, engaging in such activities during the first part of the day and revisiting it as their last action before resting. This self-reflection is not a "what to do for the day" list, but rather a thoughtful connection practice that may include meditation, prayer, or journaling around purpose and vision.

Make no mistake, intrapersonal intelligence, like that of its emotional intelligence partner, must be worked on regularly. It is perhaps one of the hardest of the intelligences to achieve. Seeking an executive coach to assist you as you travel this pathway to achieve what you want and, before that, to be clear on why you want it is one positive strategy for leaders who want to improve their engagement with and mastery of this intelligence.

What if you are set with checking your emotions and are already doing your daily assessments, journaling and reflecting on your PinLeader Path? Is there more to do? Of course! Now you need to take those sharp skills and leverage them to take the next step as a leader who can communicate a message that motivates others. This brings us to the third of the four intelligences—interpersonal intelligence.

Interpersonal Intelligence

Interpersonal intelligence builds upon emotional and intrapersonal intelligences but expands into the ability to build and maintain positive relationships. Knowing your limits and setting boundaries is one indicator of interpersonal intelligence. As a leader it is critically important that communication be at the forefront of building those relationships which demonstrate high levels of emotional intelligence. However, high levels of interpersonal intelligence require a consistent analysis of the environment and the context in which a message is sent, either verbally or nonverbally.

Think of a time when a leader verbally stated what they were going to do but acted in a way that was in complete conflict with what they stated. Their nonverbal action was in such a case a demonstration of the lack of interpersonal intelligence. The leader may have had control of their emotions when they conveyed the message; nevertheless, the statement that "actions speak louder than words" is at play here.

Understanding and relating to a specific group or audience is not a skill easily taught. It takes practice and care to make sure the message is getting out and, most importantly, understood by the audiences for which it is intended. Ordering individuals to do something and leaning on title alone rather than reason, best practice, or a deeper purpose is an indicator of a low interpersonal intelligence level.

Leaders gain interpersonal intelligence by starting their messaging journey with small groups and then listening to responses to the leader, which are based on what that group hears. If feedback comes back with more questions than anticipated, leaders make sure to rework the message in a way that uses examples that relate to those in that environment.

It is important not to take for granted that the delivery of a message one or two times will lead to it being fully received and understood. Consider different learning styles and deliver any messages through a variety of means and channels, from auditory channels (such as verbal conversations, recorded messages, or podcasts) to written forms (such as correspondence, e-mail, or reports) or using video and interactive formats (such as presentations and meetings). In marketing, repeating the critical part of a message three times helps the listener remember. However, if you want the listener to remember, understand, and act upon a message, it is most helpful to get the message delivered different ways a minimum of seven times and give the audience the ability to ask any questions each time.

The last attribute that helps demonstrate interpersonal intelligence is the ability to handle conflict. Conflict is the result of *not* being able to look through a different lens than your own in order to gain a different viewpoint or perspective. Leaders on the PinLeader Path have high interpersonal intelligence and utilize a starting position of benign intent, extending grace and the benefit of the doubt to those that they may not agree with. By examining opposing sides of position without judgement, the level of civility in the workplace also increases.

PinPoint: When faced with conflict, hesitate and then educate. Come from a place that assumes benign intent by those who may have offended and therefore reacted in a particular way. If the conflict involves those not present, advocate to shut down gossip or discussions about those individuals who are not present to engage in dialogue or discussion.

Interpersonal intelligence is an ability that can be increased. To do so will require diligence and intentional practice. It will be vital for the PinLeader to develop and maintain the skills needed and required to keep sharp in this area. But what if your team is utilizing other ways of communicating that incorporate the power of technology? What if the team is using tools that write or record messaging for them? Enter the new intelligence, known by the term artificial intelligence or AI.

Artificial Intelligence

Pins are made by machines, forged from steel and other materials that give them the strength to do the job. However, those same pins were first designed by people. The same is true of artificial intelligence. How can anything be any smarter than what it was when it was designed by its creator? It *is* possible. Enter the power of many creators, feeding into one artificial intelligence tool with an infinite variety of expressions. What starts off with a handful of solutions to solve a challenge culminates in the presentation of several breakthrough solutions. This brings new ways of looking at the phrase "many hands make light work" with the modification that that many minds make light work.

But what type of team member does an artificially sharp pin make? Could that artificial pin become a leader on its own? Is its information and guidance reliable? As artificial intelligence enhances its own wells of knowledge, so does its ability to supply a team with valuable information and guidance. Artificial intelligence is sharp and gets straight to the point, relying on the education and experience of others in order to provide solid answers. When utilized properly, AI can complement, augment, and extend each of the other three intelligences.

 PinPoint: Try utilizing AI for simple "jobs" at first. This will allow you to become acclimated with the different platforms. Never rely on one source but seek out multiple platforms and a variety of intelligence sources.

The cautionary tale is that sometimes AI does not get it right. It may be relying on inputs that have bias or misinformation. There are ways of checking on the information you glean from AI. The process is similar to the path any well-trained journalist would take. First, make sure that the source is credible. Next, get another source to check the facts and verify the results. In other words, do not rely on one AI source but several.

As in a health check up that provides news you may not have expected, it should be your position to always get a second opinion. Just as you would advocate for your health, advocate for your education. Seek different sources and check those sources. Are they motivated or backed by an agenda setting group? PinLeaders apply such critical thinking. They take nothing on face value and always consider the motivation. Once the underlying motive is identified, leaders can decide to accept the message, deny it, or simply ignore it.

Once you know which artificial intelligence sources you will use, put the scenarios into these different platforms and examine the answers provided. Check and cross check. Remember, this work all takes time. The more practice you get with AI the more useful it will become for you. One award-winning journalist I spoke with recently shared that she considered AI to be one tool but certainly not the only tool or even a primary tool for gathering information. Just as you would do when consulting another leader, you may choose to take AI's guidance and follow its direction, but you must realize that AI—or any other leader offering its intelligence— does not operate in a vacuum but as part of a greater whole.

The Rotating Door of Leaders

A Board hires Donovan to be the organization's next president. On paper, he appeared to be a good fit for the role. Donovan came highly recommended by a search firm. However, he lacks social graces, is highly political, and wants to step to the next level as soon as possible. Donovan comes with no other "pins" and decides to promote those on the former president's team who have a reputation of saying "yes" to requests but who often do not have the education and experience to fulfill their assigned scope of work.

The job titles and responsibilities for the promoted individuals (the assistant to the president, for example) are tied to the president's office without appropriate vetting or interviewing. Other leaders reporting to Donovan are considered experts and are asked to "train" these individuals and then leave their posts. Donovan has achieved a level of control and believes they are setting up the new leadership up for success.

Fast forward in time. There are external pressures from stakeholders and investors to "right the ship," so the Board asks for goals to be met and holds Donovan accountable. At this point, Donovan announces his departure, positioning his experience with the organization as a valuable stepping stone for his career. The Board does not perceive the hire as a mistake.

Instead, the Board searches and hires Janet to be president and address the areas that have received the greatest degree of scrutiny or negative public attention. The Board boasts that the new president will address the issue and solve challenging areas for the organization. Janet has neither the experience nor the education to address these additional challenging areas or pain points. Furthermore, Janet does not have the credibility to hire a leader to assist her in fulfilling the call to remedy the challenging areas.

Fast forward in time. Now, the Board asks for goals to be met in the persistent areas of challenge. Stakeholders and investors apply even greater external pressures. The Board holds Janet accountable, but now she, too, announces her departure. Janet positions this move as decision based on health concerns and claims to be stepping into a role more aligned with her skills. Again, the Board of Directors does not perceive the hiring as a potential mistake.

The Board already has credibility issues with the public. During both debacles there was a call for both the Board and each of the two prior presidents hired to resign. The Board decides to now hire Kenneth, who has been with the organization for a number of years. Kenneth was also part of the "train-them-as-they-go" approach to encourage promotion within the organization. The Board states that it now feels confident that Kenneth will be the answer as this leader has been with the organization through a number of prior presidents and has family living in the area, so is more inclined to remain in this role.

This rotating door of leaders is all too common in businesses and organizations. Organizations can guard against this scenario by reflecting on what is needed for the organization to survive and thrive, placing personal interests, friendships, and any family ties apart for what is best for the organization. Once goals are identified, seeking individuals who have the PinLeader traits and demonstrated actions in those areas most needed and required should be recruited. Organizations should seek leaders who are sharp with education and experience, have strength of character, and have the ability to get straight to the point with a plan and the ability to pivot.

PINLEADER INTERACTIVE

Join the PinLeader Path Community! Scan the QR code below to access the PinLeader Interactive. Use the following questions for further discussion and consideration.

The Case of the Rotating Door of Leaders

- What challenges do you see with this case?
- What do you think may happen during Kenneth's tenure? Why do you believe that?
- What do you think about the use of "appointments" versus the use of a "search" process?
- What advice would you give the Board?
- What would you do differently and why?

CHAPTER 3: **PinLeader Straight to the Point**

Jackie knew it was only a matter of time. Eventually the committee was going to ask her for a strategic plan. Although she had planned events and done projects before, she knew nothing about how to develop a full strategic plan. She had limited experience working with basic tools such as doing a SWOT analysis and knew she was in over her head. She had attended several meetings and even put together a small Think Tank to help develop key goals for the organization, but she wasn't sure where to go from there.

During Jackie's last performance review, her boss had said that she was looking forward to seeing the plan since Jackie had put so many hours into it. However, Jackie did not share her difficulties with her boss. Every day she worried that her boss would find out that the plan was not progressing. What made it all worse is that she seemed to be going around in circles with the Think Tank. Jackie would hold a meeting, discuss a few potential goals but she could not gain consensus with who should be responsible for what part of the plan.

Some of those who would do the work would not show up for meetings, and others had not been invited to the Think Tank from its inception. Around the table, participants would make statements agreeing that it was "everyone's job" to move the project forward. Then the Think Tank would meet again and they would be back where they started, discussing the same goals with no actionable conclusions or decisions about who would own the different parts.

Some members would even bring up scenarios that could derail a goal if it were chosen for inclusion in the plan. Jackie was restless. Based on the last meeting, so was the Think Tank and the working committee that wanted the plan, now. The project team had lost two members to other projects, and Jackie had a feeling it was more than just other commitments that led to their departure. At this point, she was unsure how long she would be able to keep this up. One thing was certain; not only was the committee counting on her to lead them in the development of a new strategic plan but her job might also be on the line.

Jackie had a number of missed opportunities to get straight to the point and secure the assistance she needed in order to get a strategic plan in place. She eventually confided in a mentor who provided helpful templates and guidance, but the Think Tank disbanded itself and Jackie was left with completing the plan on her own.

PinLeader Considerations

- What did Jackie need to do?
- Was Jackie transparent with her boss and colleagues?
- What should the Think Tank have done?
- What would be an indicator of progress in this process?

How Straight to the Point Are You?

A great leader leads people, and leading people well means knowing where you are going. Every leader has this quintessential skill. Understanding how to lead people toward the completion of a shared goal or destination is more than a skill, however. It is a practice. Similar to the attributes of being sharp and strong, PinLeaders are not born with knowing how to get straight to the point and stay on point.

Education and ongoing practice are required in order to develop and perfect skills. That practice requires discipline that only comes with the development of a solid plan. Any individual training to be the best in her respective field knows the action items to reach the goal. There are no cutting corners when it comes to planning, and each leader who can communicate her message in a clear, distinctive manner that includes the "why" will be the most effective leader.

And what if the "best laid plan" doesn't seem to be working? Most likely there was pivotable point that needed to be addressed. *How* the message is delivered by the leader does make the difference on well received the plan gets adopted.

How Curves Impact the PinLeader Path

You may have experienced hearing someone talk in a circuitous manner, not knowing where the direction of the communication or story was going to take you. Perhaps you sat politely and listened to the communication attempting to pick out the nuggets of information that were relevant to what you think the point to the story was.

Or maybe the person communicated the information in writing but in such a way that you had to read it multiple times to understand what was needed and when. Perhaps the worst scenario is that you may have sat through a meeting and realized the communication was not for you and had no relevance to your role.

Unfortunately, in each of these situations time invested in receiving such communication was not time well spent. In fact, it could be considered time wasted. Unclear communication or other actions that veer off the stated course or plan of action, such as that within an organization's strategic plan introduce a curve in the path. Such a curve can lead to confusion and disarray, not to mention throw off timelines and seriously impact an organization's ability to fulfill its mission.

Those following a PinLeader Path take the time to hone their communications skills to get straight to the point with the ultimate tool in their toolkit—a clear strategic plan. If we agree that time is valuable, then leveraging the ability to get straight to the point with relevant communication is an asset. To assist with getting to that critical point means taking the time to create a roadmap that can help guide those conversations. As with a sewing project that needs pins, a pattern, or clear instructions to guide the person undertaking the sewing project with a step by step process and plan, good leadership practice within organization requires a clear plan of action.

But how do we go about getting that strategic plan going? How do we obtain the instructions that outline the process and identifies what resources we may need? Does the journey to get straight to the point need its own plan of action?

Getting Straight to the Point

Among the three characteristics, the ability to get straight to the point and communicate clearly and consistently is often the hardest for a PinLeader to accomplish. Unlike the demonstration of strength of character or becoming sharp through education and experience, the ability to lead effectively requires an interconnected set of skills that must be put into practice over time.

Strategic planning is not occurring daily in the workplace. Hence the opportunity to practice and further hone this skill is not as readily available. In fact, it is only the act of carrying out the goals identified during the planning process that the leader touches on a daily basis. So how does a leader build this skill? Where does a team member like Jackie, who we met at the beginning of this chapter, begin? The best place to start is always in reflection.

The stage that Jackie resides in her career has impacted her approach to managing this situation. Throughout the developments with regard to the strategic plan, she only self-reflected one time and that led her to realize she did not have the skills to develop and implement the strategic plan. However, if she had obtained that skill or understood that she needed to ask for assistance by being straight to the point and transparent, she may have been able to save the Think Tank from disbanding.

To accomplish this, Jackie would have needed to build strong relationships that would allow her to lead with confidence and also request cooperation and understanding from her colleagues and direct reports as she took the time to obtain the tools she needed to lead the effort. But even if she had the tools and build the framework, what would it take to stay on course and fulfill the plan?

How do organizational plans and the personal plans of the leader work in tandem with one another? How can a PinLeader get on point and stay on point? These are the questions that must be considered by leaders who want to stay straight to the point.

Staying Straight to the Point

There comes a time when the planning phase is complete and it is time for the plan to be implemented. PinLeaders have clear direction. They consistently communicate to their teams and with the organization about the relevance of each goal. They regularly outline key responsibilities that each department or group has to implement the plan.

This move toward implementation is made with an understanding that each plan has a life cycle. Similarly, the goals set within the plan also have associated timelines. The best case scenario is that resources are put in place, responsible agents are identified, measurables are noted, action items are assigned to goals, and timetables are set.

But what happens if leaders have their own career aspirations and plans that may or may not include the current organization? Leaders then take their own agendas and plans and overlay them on top of the organization they are responsible for currently. In such a case, leaders are lacking strength of character. They are not engaging in getting straight to the point and have placed service to themselves above service to the organization and its stated mission.

The best scenario is similar to our discussion of matching the right pin for the job. Those leaders that follow the PinLeader Path listen to the organization and do their own self reflection to see whether missions and visions align. In one example, a leader was deciding if he wanted to be in a leadership role with a company that made tobacco products. This leader did not philosophically support products manufactured and sold by the company. This created an internal conflict since the leader believed he wanted this opportunity solely because of the career step it provided. In this scenario, what would be the best path forward?

If we are following the PinLeader way of thinking, the leader should not take the role because he was not taking the job for his alignment with the organization but merely to make a career move. How could this leader keep straight on point if he was unable to be transparent about those qualities he believed contributed to a great organization? How can he motivate and inspire others if he was not passionate about the organization?

Let's look at the situation when the leader and the organizational plans are aligned. There are still considerations to be made. At times, for example, organizations loop in a constant state of planning but never reach their goals. A leader comes into place, creates a plan, begins to implement, and then leaves before completing the implementation of the plan. The next leader comes, rejects the prior plan, creates a new plan, begins to implement that plan, and then leaves. Thus the cycle of perpetual planning occurs. Who loses in this scenario? The organization and, in some cases, the leader.

The strongest leaders hold a philosophy that just because they did not create the plan does not mean that it is a poor plan. PinLeaders utilize their sharpness and rely on all their intelligences, in this case their emotional and intrapersonal intelligences, to determine what may be able to be kept or enhanced from current plans. Understanding the historical perspective is a key differentiator between PinLeaders and those leaders who are not willing or able to examine the fuller context and accept plans that are not their own. This brings us to another critical juncture along the PinLeader Path: looking to the past to build a bridge to the future.

Looking Back to Push Forward

To get where you are going, you have to know where you have been. To move things forward, it is often helpful to look to the past. Great strategic plans do not occur over night. Nor are they built in a bubble. They are entrenched in history.

The best strategic plans have a foundation that has been carefully curated and shaped by experienced hands. Those hands often belong to a PinLeader who has a breadth of knowledge about what has worked and what has not worked in the past for the organization. The challenges, the successes, and the historical context of what has occurred must all be considered so that a new path can be forged. Each of these nuances inform the best plans for forward progress.

Some may ask why it is necessary or desirable to forge a new path. Every plan creates a new path, even when that plan has been based off of a prior plan. One fact remains clear: until science proves otherwise we cannot time travel. However, what we can do is learn from the past. When it comes to strategic planning and staying on path, it is important to embrace all parts of the historical context, including those that may make some within an organization uncomfortable.

Facing the truth that some goals did not work is inevitable. However, the recognition and acknowledgment that certain action items attached to previous goals were not fulfilled due to budget constraints does not mean that the entire plan was flawed. It simply means that the overall plan had goals or actions that were too ambitious for the organization *at that point in time*.

Reflecting on those unmet goals should not be seen as harmful. Nor is it a criticism of past leadership. Leaders who want to move an organization forward should look at the context of when and why those goals were put in place. This looking back is time well spent and supports forward momentum with strategic goals and objectives.

PinPoint: Leaders should not be outwardly critical of past leadership. If they were hired to help get the organization back on track, leaders should demonstrate a healthy respect or those who previously led the organization.

Leaders who are new to an organization should do their own research to uncover past plans. You may find those plans in your own office, in areas led by a chief of staff, or in departments such as human resources or finance. Each plan should be carefully reviewed and considered. Where possible, interview those who were part of the initial development of those plans. Knowledge is power.

There's nothing better than institutional memory to help with context. Glean past plans and processes to gain the perspective needed to move forward from where you are now with a full understanding of where the organization has been.

Crooked Paths Make for Long Journeys

Now let's assume that you have gathered up all the historical pieces to the previous plan's creation. However, you find that a scorecard on progress was missing. The tracking you expected to find was not in place. You attempt to find more information but to no avail. What becomes even more clear is that the mission of the institution does not match the goals set within the plan. The goals seem to have been set to a broader agenda, and it is unclear how those goals would advance the organization.

In other words, the plan went off track with a previous leader who lost sight of the organization's purpose. The leader was well intentioned but something unexpected happened. She understood the plan but there was a challenge that got in the way of fulfilling the timeline, so a modified goal was set. Consequently, the leader began to diverge little by little from the path and plan agreed upon. After all, that leader created the plan. Doesn't she have the right to change it? The management team that worked with the leader to implement the plan seemed to have understood as well. After all, the management team hired the leader to create the plan in the first place.

What if, as you attempt to gain a historical perspective and context, you uncover that the team did not agree to changes made to the plan? What if the originally agreed upon outcomes were different from those which you see reflected in the version of the plan you have? Perhaps the former leader reduced or increased the measurable objectives to take into account the degree of challenge in meeting those objectives. Many of the original team members who worked on parts of the plan are long gone along with the former leader. What happens now?

Deviating from plans happens more often than what one might expect. It can be easily justified, especially when it is due to an unforeseen circumstance. But what is the result? Does an extenuating circumstance make it okay to veer off course with the stated plan? No. In fact, leaders must hold themselves accountable to a plan even when others will not. Pivoting is not the problem but *how* that pivot is handled is.

 PinPoint: Organizations that have adopted plans that have deviated from their mission may have justified this approach of moving forward at any cost, believing any plan is better than no plan. Leaders should be aware of the danger of deviating from the plan. It is vital to maintain a desire and commitment to keep to the organization's stated mission.

What are the consequences of deviating from the stated course of action? Any sewing project requires the purchase of materials and the choice of a pattern to follow. In a leadership capacity within an organization, once you start to deviate from the original project, the resource commitment will change. This includes what kind of pins will be required and, most importantly, how many pins will be needed for the job.

To further illustrate this point, think about a sewing project that needs a number of pins to hold the fabric in place. Pins that are sharp, strong, and straight are the most desirable in any project. Even so, results may vary depending on the project. Different fabrics have different strengths. If multiple fabrics are used or fabrics are layered, this may result in a pin that is easily bent.

As a leader your first goal should be to understand what the project calls for. The next step is to select the right pin for the job. Not having the right leaders in place or not having enough leaders who have the full picture of where the organization has come from and where it is heading will make reaching any goal a longer stretch. Assessing each leader and then determining the right number of leaders for the job are intricacies that require yet another layer of planning.

The moral of this sewing story? You cannot over plan.

Staying Present to Plan for the Future

So now all the historical information has been gathered. What are the next steps? This is where the leader who follows the PinLeader Path can shine by putting all their other skills into motion. Leaders see the opportunity for moving forward by looking to their current team for the prospect of future leaders who can rise into greater leadership through their role in executing the plan.

While assessing their teams, leaders keep a diligent eye out and even look into other departments for talent. Ultimately, the PinLeader Path helps those who have the potential to carry out different aspects of the plan to balance their responsibilities to the department or area of the organization to which they are assigned with their role in helping to implement the strategic plan.

Timetables for plan creation vary, depending upon the amount of information needed to begin the process. After the plan implementation begins, a review to check for the achievement of short term goals and wins should be carried out. The review will build momentum and goodwill for the plan, especially if there have been multiple plans created by former leaders.

PinLeaders can solicit the assistance of an external experienced strategic plan consultant to help them lead meetings, to get the process started, and to keep notes that capture key ideas and insights from those who are vested in the process. A Chief of Staff role could potentially help manage the strategic planning process, but only if this leader has the expertise.

Each step of the process needs careful planning and consistent communication. It is important that each of the ten strategic planning steps be led by the project leader. Effective leadership does not necessarily mean that the leader will personally take on each of the actions required to achieve each goal but bring others to the table who can.

Pinning Steps for Strategic Planning

These are the ten steps that successful leaders follow when developing a strategic plan.

1. **Determine the departments or areas** that will be most impactful for and impacted by your strategic plan. Invite a responsible leader to represent that area and be part of a Strategic Plan Team (SPT). The composition of the SPT can be executive leadership but does not have to be as long as executive leadership is aware of who represents them in the planning team.

2. **Hold plan parameter meetings.** Create an agenda that clearly outlines timelines and outcomes. The meetings can be led by an external consultant or include other third party support.

3. **Following each meeting, provide minutes to the SPT.** Outline next actions assigned to specific SPT members. The PinLeader should not be listed as responsible agent for every action; rather, specific team members should be assigned to key deliverables.

4. **Create an outline with goals,** with action items for each goal. Also include responsible parties, timelines for completion, measurable objectives (should be in

percentage or number), and any financial or human resources required for completion.

5. **Create a letter of commitment** for the plan and have leadership sign it. The letter would be written by the organization's president with different parts, to include but not be limited to the following: the reasons behind creating the plan and how the leader supports it, the importance that each department plays in the plan's overall implementation, trends in the industry that may be impacting the organization, and an inspirational quote or phrase that speaks to the urgency of the plan and the need to work together to meet the goals outlined in the plan.

6. **Publish the final plan** and disseminate the proposed plan in order to solicit feedback. Share the plan with both internal and external partners or the community as a whole.

7. **Measure and report. Provide scorecards** at regular intervals, noting whether and to what degree measurables are being met. Also detail any deviations to the plan and reasons for any change.

8. **Communicate successes.** Openly acknowledge any challenges.

9. **Hold periodic listening sessions** that encourage questions about the plan's progress and gather input from across the organization.

10. **Recognize that the plan will have a completion date.** Prepare your team and lay the groundwork for the next plan during the last six months of the prior plan.

The Future Design

As noted in step ten of *Pinning Steps for Strategic Planning*, planning is also about the future. A leader on the PinLeader Path knows that plans have a lifespan and that those plans may change based on a number of factors that the leader cannot control or manage. Knowing what is and what is not in their sphere of control is a key differentiator between fair leaders and those who are exceptional. When things go awry, the exceptional PinLeader does not take the easy road and look for someone to blame.

When it comes to evaluating leaders within an organization, a key question for executive leadership should always be whether the organization's challenges would have been present with or without that particular leader in charge. If the answer is that this challenge would have occurred in either case, then the leader cannot be held solely responsible for any failure.

Forecasting

One of the major challenges for an organization will be its own forecasting. If you ask some of the most successful leaders, you will find that they have not always been able to hold to or meet their forecasts. They may have had a solid plan, but a circumstance, either personal or professional, has led to a change in direction.

Good leaders know that a circumstance of some sort is coming. Great leaders prepare in advance for that circumstance and use it to their advantage when it appears. The fact is that good and great leaders cannot always know in advance if a certain change will need to be implemented. What effective leaders do know is that change is inevitable. As such, they have contingency plans in place that allow them to prepare for the most likely circumstances.

During a period of change, an organization can turn to two useful data points that can impact the successful navigation of that change:

1. the source of the change, and
2. the reaction of a poor leader.

With an understanding that change is inevitable and happening on a continual basis, an organization's leadership understands that the source of the change is not controllable. This understanding requires the organization to eliminate as many factors as possible that are not predictive. One of these factors that can be controlled is the organization's ability to minimize the behaviors of a poor leader.

The PinLeader Path includes an understanding that the strategic plan is a living document. A strong leader is ready and able to pivot based on changing circumstances. The strongest organizations ensure their leaders are prepared to adapt to unforeseen circumstances and equipped to lead their teams to do the same.

 PinPoint: Strategic planning is not fortune telling and leaders do not have crystal balls. A plan is created to be followed, but no leader can predict the future or guarantee good fortune. Strategic plans are one tool utilized by those who follow the PinLeader Path. These plans provide guidance for effective resource allocation and for measurement of the organization's success.

The Pivot

A Gallup poll found that managers account for at least 70 percent of discrepancies in employee engagement scores across all business levels. The same poll found that companies failed to choose the right talent for the job

82 percent of the time.[10] Imagine that a change comes, and imagine that change comes where there is a lack of engagement within organizational teams and the wrong leader is at the helm. In such cases, a pivot will be necessary.

> **PinPoint:** Anticipating change is vital, but the ability to see and state that change is already here is the true mark of those on the PinLeader Path. How a leader reacts to change is something that can be anticipated. Only the prepared leader will be able to pivot quickly and effectively.

This is similar to choosing the wrong pin and placing that pin in the wrong part of the fabric. When an unexpected pull comes out of nowhere, the fabric unravels. The likelihood at such a point is that the project will fall apart before a seam gets put in place. From a personal standpoint, great leaders may have a situation that forces them to step down. The prepared leader will have a successor who has a full understanding of the plan in place and is ready to pick the project up and move it forward. If the unexpected pull or a challenge to the organization comes, the leader will be well positioned to acknowledge the new circumstance and propose a new direction.

> **PinPoint:** Those on the PinLeader Path do not attempt to control a circumstance they did not create it. They make sure to look at all angles to produce the best case scenario and a win-win for the organization, their team, and themselves, in that order.

---

[10] Randall J. Beck and Jim Harder. "Why Great Managers are so Rare." Gallup. https://www.gallup.com/workplace/231593/why-great-managers-rare.aspx

Planning for the Pivot

Any time a need to pivot presents itself, it's important to plan for change to occur. How can you do that? Sometimes it is not the plan that should demand a leader's full attention but a closer look at the *process* which got the plan created. If a leader examines how the making of the plan unfolded and continues to periodically revisit those processes in order to update the plan according to meet current changes, the plan may not have to be recreated every few years but simply updated.

As with any project, you may come to trust one pattern creator or a strategic plan developer more than another. *Figure 2: The Strategic Plan Pivot Change Model* on the following page outlines the importance of scorecards and shows the impact of change leading to periodic revisions. This is noted in Step 7 of *Pinning Steps for Strategic Planning* outlined earlier in this chapter. The planning process is the first step leading to the plan and eventually the scorecard. The pivot required at the moment of change impacts not only the plan but also the process used to develop or arrive at the plan.

If a leader has a budget shortfall and the strategic plan is already in place, then she must go back to the process in order to build this change into the strategic plan. However, a number of leaders do not do this, and it is a critical mistake. The assumption is to simply make the fix and then proceed with the plan as it stands. But by just changing the plan, the leader loses the opportunity to engage with the stakeholders who were part of the original planning process, essentially leaving the team out of the equation.

In the best of circumstances, a leader will gather the information in the process phase and allow that to lead them into a revision of the plan. Once the leader has the revised plan, she will need to periodically check to see if it is successful. This process requires the development of a scorecard.

Remember, the scorecard is measuring the effectiveness of the implementation plan and not the pivot or change. Modifications to the plan should be made based on measured results, with those results leading back to each of the action steps. In this model, the plan is impacted by change, but the process and any needed modifications to the plan are made based on measured results.

FIGURE 2: THE STRATEGIC PLAN PIVOT CHANGE MODEL

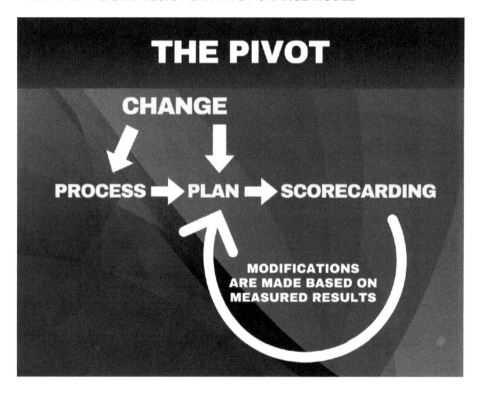

Evaluating Leaders in a Pivot

Overall, a pivot is an opportunity to separate good leaders from great ones. Options for responding well to new circumstances may include repositioning or expanding the plan. Or the PinLeader may propose that the organization venture onto a new path with the potential for greater growth along this new trajectory. The adage of making lemonade out of lemons applies here. It is all in the messaging and the way the communication about the pivot is delivered.

Teams watch how a leader responds to new circumstances. The pivot must be embraced, and original and revised plans must address critical "what if" scenarios. Forecasting for unanticipated circumstances is the best approach, and a strategic plan that includes such contingencies will help build the credibility needed to gain momentum and drive the project forward.

 PinPoint: Following the PinLeader Path means that a leader is always meeting with different departments to listen to their challenges and goals to ensure any concerns about change are addressed.

Think back on the beginning of the chapter with Jackie and her challenges with getting a plan created. There were endless meetings, a Think Tank that went round and round but never reached decisions, and a number of scenarios without group consensus or proper leadership. Even if a goal was put in the plan, these circumstances were sure to derail meaningful progress.

The future is the least of Jackie's concerns when she is struggling with the day to day and decisions about what to do to move forward. Jackie needs professional development, but until she gets that she needs a mentor who can help her. The process must start with her being transparent with her boss.

She needs to ask for assistance, which may include an outside consultant. She must take concrete steps to organize the Think Tank with clear agendas that keep the group on track. She must ensure the possible scenarios and situations that may derail a goal are considered in advance. To do this, she needs to ensure everything from the meetings is captured so she and the team can take steps in the right direction. The last thing Jackie should do is to allow potential roadblocks brought up by team members to be a hindrance to moving forward.

A Plan to Nowhere

David felt the excitement of knowing that he had finally achieved his goal of becoming president of his organization. He knew he had just a few months to determine what needed to be done to move the organization toward its goals. The board explained that they would back his decisions and asked him to come up with a plan that they could share with the community.

David had left the last organization and a number of associates behind. He had contemplated bringing some with him but a number of his prior team members did not want to work for him anymore. He was not used to writing plans himself, but he had emphasized his ability to produce a solid plan to the board. David believed he could do nearly everyone's senior level job. He was equally confident that he could hire someone to do what was needed, so he began the process of finding a right-hand leader. The first assignment for the new associate? To write the strategic plan.

After hiring Anthony, David promised to help Anthony secure his own presidency but only after his successful completion of the organization's strategic plan. Anthony agreed. Several meetings took place, and groups across the organization were engaged in the process. Each group set their own goals and key performance measures (KPMs) to accompany their stated goals. An outline was created. More than a year passed, and the framework was completed. Writing to fill in the details took another three months. Two years later, the plan was deemed complete.

However, the plan had a major flaw. It was so long and convoluted that David could not seem to follow what Anthony presented. When asked simple questions by board members, David gave generic responses without substance or understanding of where the goals had originated. Since the measurements were also created by individual teams and departments and each had set their own parameters, many of the goals and KPMs did not make sense across departments and for the good of the organization.

David knew there were flaws, but Anthony was starting to gain credibility because he had engaged with the departments during the planning process. Concerned about being outshined by Anthony, David fulfilled his side of the agreement. He helped Anthony secure the professional development required so he could seek out and find his own presidency. David made do with the plan but soon began to pursue a new position of his own—a presidency at a larger and more important institution. After leaving for what would be considered a lateral leadership opportunity, David's legacy of leading the organization was left in question.

What was also left behind was a plan that the next president deemed unachievable and disconnected from the organization's mission. The plan was scrapped, and a new cycle of strategic planning was started. The plan had taken two years to develop, which was a year longer than what the board expected. Unfortunately the excitement originally generated to create a plan was now dampened and those in the new strategic plan process were less than optimistic about seeing any plan come to its fruition.

PINLEADER INTERACTIVE

Join the PinLeader Path Community! Scan the QR code below to access the PinLeader Interactive. Use the following questions for further discussion and consideration.

The Case of the Plan to Nowhere

- What could have David done differently?
- What were the positives of the strategic planning process?
- What do you think the Board could have done?
- What do you think will happen next in this organization? Why do you think that?

CHAPTER 4: **PinLeader Strength**

It was too much to handle. Weeks earlier John had learned that budget cuts were inevitable and he had been trying to avoid any conversation about it ever since. He had thought about how he was going to deliver the news that there would be yet another round of cuts to each team member. He had lost sleep over it.

John had played the conversation over and over in his mind. He had fought for his team, explaining to management how his team's perceived shortcomings and failures were the result of another department's failures. How he never had indicated his team could hit the sales number in the first place. How others on his team would protest. How no one would stand for the cut. But the day had come, and still there had been no change. John was going to have to tell his team. He had no choice. He would be forced to call in each team member and share the difficult truth of the situation.

Worst of all, management had asked him to talk about only the good and to sell this move as a necessary part of doing business. John was not sure if he wanted to "sell" anything. In fact, he was not convinced the budget cuts were needed at all. He didn't feel prepared, and he did not want to let go of any department members he had worked with for the last decade. This is not what he signed up for when he took the leadership role. It had not been what he expected. Not at all. Not even the online professional development course the company had made him take had prepared him for this.

The more John thought about it, waiting until some of the staff had taken their vacations to tell them the news sounded like a much better plan. The delay was in contradiction of what his supervisor had told him to do, which was to deliver the news by the end of the week. But wouldn't waiting be the smarter way to handle the situation?

PinLeader Considerations

- What do you think John should do?

- Should he postpone the conversations or confront the situation without delay?

- What are the challenges or potential downsides to what John is about to do or not do?

- What do you think should happen instead?

Credibility and the Strength to Lead

John is being called to do what many leaders often find themselves doing —making a difficult decision that negatively impacts those they care about. In such situations, leaders following the PinLeader Path work hard to integrate reason with purpose. They rely on their inner strength. They can only accomplish what needs to be done when they have earned the credibility to do so, and credibility comes through their consistent demonstration of the strength to lead.

Strength of character counts. It is worth so much to those who are in leadership positions in today's fast-paced organizations where change is a constant. Leaders who have not developed their strength quickly fold when faced with difficult and demanding situations. This is why strength is one of the three traits of the PinLeader.

How Strong Are You?

The strength of any pin depends upon what it is made of. Poorly constructed pins made of plastic break at the first sign of resistance. The best pins, and all great leaders on the PinLeader Path are made of steel. Leaders know how to celebrate appropriately. They encourage staff and teams even when there seems to be a lot standing in the way of the success of the whole team or individual members. The strongest leaders have the capacity to respond with empathy when jobs are lost. They learn to lead with conviction and character, not force of will.

> **PinPoint:** Do not confuse strength with force. Leaders who attempt to force constituents or team members into a certain action by instituting negative consequences often find their teams following their directions but the team members unwilling or unconvinced when it comes to influencing their peers to follow suit.

Top Pin Choice

Effective leaders have the strength of character to create synergy and successfully enlist team members to follow their lead requires tenacity and a determination to remain strong under the constant pressures of decision making. Strong leaders must be able to hold a team together in the wake of adversity. PinLeaders find a way to push through the toughness of material that makes up the fabric of an organization and at the same time work with that fabric to move things forward.

The strength of a leader is defined by that leader's ability to take on new challenges. By drawing on character while maintaining, sustaining, and even enriching the fabric of a team and the organization as a whole, the strong leader navigates the choppy waters of change with finesse if not ease. A pin is selected based on its ability to get the job done and, essentially, to hold the fabric of a team or an organization together. Weak pins may have the ability to remain in place for a period of time but are not dependable for the long term.

Think about the leaders who had a number of character flaws and the ways those leaders can often create more problems because they do not have the strength of character to sustain success and to lead effectively within a given culture. The strength of character is what sets the great leaders apart from mediocre leaders. They are strong inside and out and can lead their teams through the most difficult of transitions. They know the secret of leveraging their internal skill set and drawing on the strengths of those around them.

Spheres of Influence

At their tops, many pins are round, some of them sporting a colorful sphere that makes the pin easier to see. Believe it or not, that round top has another, more important purpose. The small sphere is created to help the person using the pin apply force and thereby accomplish the task at hand with greater ease and effectiveness. This round top typically stays smooth. The spherical shape allows anyone to pick up the pin by its rounded top. Its purpose is to help leverage the strength of the pin.

Leaders achieve leverage in the same way, relying on their own sphere of influence. The best leaders fully understand that they have power to lead. They know they need to leverage their own strengths as well as the strengths of their team members to get work done. However, PinLeaders understand that they do have limits to that influence.

 PinPoint: A leader's sphere of influence changes over time. The sphere of influence may expand and contract based on the focus of projects and scope of responsibility.

The PinLeader also knows when supervisors or those in charge want or need them to pivot. PinLeaders continue to cultivate strong relationships and build their network. They continually build trust with the teams they manage through authentic leadership and connection. They possess attributes such as loyalty, empathy, respect, ethics, morals, and care.

They demonstrate a sense of fairness and justice. Above all else, they remain alert and aware of the boundaries of their influence and become adept at knowing how much pressure to apply in any given situation.

Strength of Character

Strong leaders use glass half full logic versus glass half empty reasoning. They know that it is all too easy to view circumstances negatively. They also understand that a positive outlook is not about denial of the facts. Leaders who demonstrate strength of character are confident and stay positive on purpose. Strong leaders know that negative reinforcement simply does not work. They motivate team members through clear communication and positive expectation. They lead by example.

Think of a time when a leader was asked to obtain consensus on an area or topic that was perceived as negative. Was the leader successful? Why or why not? Did she demand the team follow them without question? Or did she coach the team to potential positive outcomes? Preparation and transparency, along with sharing pertinent facts and insights in a timely manner, builds credibility needed for a strong leader to penetrate the dense fabric of negative perceptions. If leaders do not know what the truth is, they will garner respect by being strong enough to admit they do not know. Integrity goes a long distance with the team.

 PinPoint: Lying to teams may buy time but eventually the team will discover the truth of a situation. Pursue pathways to truth whenever possible. Be honest when answers are not available.

The strength of those who follow the PinLeader Path is rooted in truth and integrity. Teams and organizations will trust a leader when they know that leader is fair and honest. The pattern present in the case of those on the PinLeader Path is one where all three of these attributes—truth, honesty, and integrity—are woven together seamlessly. It is not linear, one attribute followed by the other, but rather circular. Each of the key attributes blends into the other two. The attributes build on one another. Like a sphere, they expand and grow the individual leader and build up those around that leader.

Influence gained by truth is strength. Strength gained by a commitment to truth, honesty, and integrity at all times will give a strong leader a greater degree of influence. Together these essential qualities make up the character of a leader. They are a key determining factor in that leader's ultimate success.

So what are those steps to developing those qualities? To begin with, it is essential to have a set of boundaries that you will not cross. The effective leader will identify clear priorities that are based in and always lead back to their own personal brand of values. There is a saying that if a person will lie, they will also steal. "Stretching" the truth to win over a client is not integrity. Overselling your capabilities in hopes it will work out in the end is not honest. Confidence in knowing you can meet the need if you put in the work is integrity. Take the first steps to write down your values and share them with at least one other person. The value of this level of accountability cannot be overstated.

Another vital step is when you are faced with the "zig" or "zag" moment of being honest or just going along with others is to pause and consider the consequences to both sides of that equation. Knowing in advance what it will cost you or what can be gained by either option is important. The PinLeader Path demands that you stay straight and act in accordance with your stated principles.

How Fragility Impacts the PinLeader Path

To be fragile does not mean that leaders are weak from their very core. In all likelihood a specific circumstance has brought this leader to a place where reexamining their actions is vital—not only to the organization but also to themselves personally and professionally. Burn out is inevitable if the leader does not take care of themselves and if they do not get the support they need. But a fragile leader can be the invitation to creative solutions. Enter the opportunity for more pins!

More Pins Please

The strength of a pin to hold fabric pieces together is usually tested and found to be most effective when there is a balance and understanding of what any one pin can do. When you add more dimensions to existing projects, add more projects, and add more goals, there is no feasible way one "pin" can do it all. At some time during the life cycle of a project or organization the need to change out PinLeaders or to add more than one leader to the team occurs.

Those on a PinLeader Path are strong but they too have their bending and breaking points. We will explore this further in Chapter 6, "The Push." Recognizing limitations at the outset saves time and can potentially prevent financial loss for the organization. Strong leaders are self-aware and know their limitation. They do not overpromise. Instead, they put measures in place to guard their well-being and their reputation. These measures include time limits set for work and keeping distances from other leaders that do harm in speaking ill will against others. If the leader is honest and self-aware and the organization ethically adheres to reasonable expectation boundaries, success is likely.

Cultures that foster adding multiple leaders who follow the PinLeader Path are forward thinking organizations. When there is a complex project with different parts that must be brought together, multiple pins, strategically spaced, are required. The placement and role of these pins must be optimized and defined in advance to achieve the desired result. Hiring multiple leaders to lead key departments is a common scenario in today's organizations. By orienting leaders toward a common purpose and goal, the organization increases the likelihood that those leaders will encourage and inspire their teams to work toward the common goal.

Talent Development

In addition to expanding the leadership team when needed, strong organizations develop the talent they already have. When an organization invests its resources in building the pins it already has, it ultimately creates a deep bench. That deep bench, in turn, creates a strong foundation for effective succession planning. This way of thinking helps with recruitment. In addition, it is an attractor to those who already have or are developing the PinLeader characteristics of being sharp, strong, and straight to the point.

Talent is too valuable to fail to develop it properly. It is not wise for any organization to approach recruitment and professional development in a way that results in recruitment being the first line item to be cut in the budget. The need to develop talent is especially true when the competition is watching and being intentional about recruiting top talent to grow their own organizations. Leaders who treat time management, fiscal management, and professional development as top priorities do extremely well.

PinPoint: Don't be the organization that serves as the "training ground" for the next generation of leaders. Be the organization that trains the next generation of leaders who want to stay.

Getting Strong

An example of how strength is demonstrated comes from leadership author John Kotter. In his seminal book *Leading Change*, Kotter explains that management and leadership are two very different concepts. He writes that leaders motivate and provide clear direction while management controls and plans with detailed steps. Kotter indicates that between 10 and 30 percent of successful change happens in the management bucket while an overwhelming 70 to 90 percent of successful change occurs in the leadership bucket.[11]

Between the two vantage points of the micromanager and an effective leader are significant degrees of differences. Some leaders would rather create policy and over-manage a group rather than attempt to find ways to motivate the group. This is because it is easier to dictate a rule than to take the time to build relationships and trust. In other words, managing the team is less work than leading a team. An example of this would be a manager who creates a policy that outlines consequences for non-approved time off. Contrast this with a leader who shares how each team member is contributing to organizational or department goals and thanks team members, assuring them that their full involvement and presence is needed.

By seeking to be a strong leader, those who are committed to the PinLeader Path ensure their teams are set to thrive and not just survive through any change or crisis. The PinLeader's sphere of influence

---

[11] John P. Kotter, *Leading Change*, Harvard Business Review Press (2012): p. 28.

supports them to work for the good of the organization. Their demonstrated strength of character helps build a positive reputation for themselves, the teams they lead, and the organization.

Simply put, PinLeaders are 100 percent aligned with effective change because they are strong enough to manage their teams through that change. Strong leaders get stronger when they dare to remain at the helm and stave off the temptation to get lost in the detail or be satisfied with managing projects and teams. PinLeaders know the difference between management and leadership, and they lead for change. But strong leaders are never satisfied to rest on their laurels. Instead, they take action to stay strong throughout their tenure with an organization.

Staying Strong

Imagine being asked to put on a blindfold. Told that you have been given the strongest pin among a bunch of pins that are placed in one hand, you are then handed two pieces of fabric in the other hand. Then you are asked to start pinning the fabrics together. You may start to feel your way to determine how to bring the pin to the correct area. You may even ask for further direction or perhaps ask someone nearby to use their hands to help guide you. Regardless of how you decide to complete the task and no matter how strong the pin, it does not take long to realize you are going into this situation without what you may be accustomed to having—your clear sight.

In a similar fashion, at any given time in their tenure, leaders may not have all the necessary information to complete a task or lead a team. They may have the strongest work ethic, possess the necessary character attributes to lead, be highly regarded by other leaders, and be wholly committed to the mission. However, even leaders on the PinLeader Path are likely to fail if they go into the situation with nothing more than blind faith.

 PinPoint: Loyalty does not mean blind faith. Leaders entering new positions should do their research and tread carefully.

Do Your Research

Think of an instance when a leader came into a role and within a few short months reported that the situation was worse than what she initially understood. The leader may claim she was not given all the facts. Or perhaps she would indicate that she needs more time to right the ship due to the additional challenges that have been uncovered. In many cases, this leader entered the situation trusting it would all work out. She failed to do her due diligence.

Does this make the leader any less valuable than when she was hired? What if she was recruited by a headhunter and information about the situation at the new employer was intentionally withheld from the headhunter by the hiring organization? Whatever the details, it is often prudent to withhold judgement of a leader who says they need more time and to provide her with grace.

Some organizations who bring in new presidents or CEOs refer to this as a "honeymoon" period. These leaders know they can count on the support of those who hired them to help them understand the full scope of both current challenges and the big picture vision for the ideal. Unethical organizations will purposefully withhold this information. They may even attempt to blame the failures on the new leadership. For these reasons, any leader coming into an organization should be cautious and aware. Research as much as possible before you say yes so that you can have the most successful tenure possible.

PinPoint: Executives, boards, and hiring managers should be clear on expectations with the new leader. Being candid and transparent about the challenges the organization is facing helps the entire team to be more successful.

Hard as Nails or a Strong Pin?

Some may ask why not be hard as nails? Nails are tough and can be pounded into a board and hold an entire house together. Nails have that specific purpose. Yet, the sheer force required to pound hard enough to join two pieces of wood together is not the kind of effort any leader should need to exert. To then have to pry the nail out requires even more energy. Sure, a "tough as nails" attitude may demonstrate true grit, but it does not contribute to self-care or the care of one's team.

Effective leaders should have care for themselves and their team top of mind at all times. The ability to be self aware is critically important. There is never a need for a leader to lead in a situation where they know they cannot hold the fabric together. Strong leaders are discerning. They have learned how to be exacting in leading their teams and know there is such a thing as too much force. They place a high value on their own well-being and the well-being of those they lead.

Self-care includes a generous dose of patience. That patience should be extended to team members who need more support, more time to fulfill their obligations, and a deeper understanding about what needs to be completed. The seasoned and effective leaders develop and maintain patience with themselves and with those they lead.

The PinLeader Path does not always lead to immediate wins, and those following this path should not measure their success based solely on wins. Not everyone within the team sees or understands what leadership is doing or why they are doing it, but when leaders demonstrate patience and persistence, a level of care and empathy are more likely to be present.

Developing strength in leadership takes time and dedication. Leaders know where they are in their daily practice of self-awareness. They create a plan for their professional development in order to hone and integrate new skills. The strongest leaders advocate for themselves and freely acknowledge that there are areas for improvement. In other words, to get strong means to know one's weaknesses and to continue on a path of learning and growth.

 PinPoint: Know that there is a life cycle to every leader. Smart organizations look for new ways to engage the leader, ultimately helping to keep the leader current and hold boredom at bay.

Pins have advantages over nails. When nails are used and then removed, there can be no permanency or sustainability. Whatever structure was built is most likely going to fall. When a pin is used to hold pieces of fabric together, it is understood that the pin will not always be there. This is an interim step to the final goal. At some point, the intention should be to sew the fabric together and then to remove the pin to create a more permanent joining together of the fabric. (See Chapter 5, "Why Some Cultures Thrive and Others Die.") This is the advantage of the PinLeader Path.

What Is This Pin Made Of?

How do you know if strength is present in a leader? Think of how many times character is called into question in the workplace. Conversely, consider how often a leader has done well by sticking through a challenging time. There are leaders who push through challenges based on their desire to remain with a particular employer.

Perhaps that leader has nowhere else to go or he does not know what to do next in his career. Perhaps that leader does not have a plan. If the leader does have a plan, he may know that, with time and carefully placed resources, he can implement that plan and be successful within the organization.

We opened this chapter by considering the differences between a pin made of plastic versus one constructed from steel. At some point, all leaders will feel they may not have been as strong as they should have been in a circumstance. While the strongest pins may be made of steel, this does not mean that they cannot be worn out. The ability to evaluate past weak points and to course correct is essential. Sometimes rest is required.

Rest and Renewal

Every pin can be overused. Solving the same problem or issue time and time again wears on anyone. If a pin is used time and time again to penetrate into the fabric and hold the fabric together, the strength of that pin will eventually diminish. This is true with those that follow the PinLeader Path as well.

Every great leader needs rest. Whether it is to recharge with a vacation or just to take a break from the day-to-day grind, a successful leader sets aside time for rest and renewal. They plan for such periods of rest in advance, preparing a space for another leader to step in while they are away.

 PinPoint: Every pin needs to sit in the pin cushion and rest at some point. Leaders need time to recharge and reflect after the completion of a project. They need rest in order to prepare for the next challenge. With these periods of rest, they can then return to creating, leading change, and being a positive role model for their teams.

The ability to recharge makes for better leaders—and better team members. It leads to better results. Those with poor mental health due to exhaustion make poor decisions that ultimately cost an organization not only financial resources but also exemplary employees. But maybe the thought of taking that vacation seems impossible.

 PinPoint: Once leaders understand their worth and recognize demands on their time will never cease, their primary responsibility is to set boundaries or to move on from their current role.

Have you ever worried about taking a vacation? Are you concerned about what others may think if you enjoy time off? Has a suggestion been made to you to set an example by working longer hours or taking on more projects and a heftier workload? These are other ways of wearing out a pin. Those who are not sure they can "risk" taking a break for fear of being replaced are in all likelihood residing in a poor culture. Such a culture is unsustainable.

 PinPoint: By following the PinLeader Path and taking a stand in a respectful but determined way, leaders protect themselves and their team members. Remember, your team is always watching and observing these interactions. There is the potential for them to develop positive perceptions of you as they observe the example you set. A positive culture pays dividends when it comes to job performance and long-term satisfaction.

PinLeader Protection

All of this comes down to that noted sphere of influence. When leaders take reasonable measures to protect themselves, other leaders and team members take notice. Leaders need to understand that the best leaders on their team have options. They also need to realize that leaders who rise to greatness need space to operate, to demonstrate their capability, and to lean into their greatness.

Once a leader's sphere of influence expands to the degree that other leaders want to follow them, it is critical that the organization recognize this shift and do all they can to engage and encourage that leader to heartily embrace a PinLeader Path. Before long, more leaders will surround the originator following such a path and be influenced by that leader. At this point, the cycle starts over again.

> **PinPoint:** Great leaders choose carefully what spheres of influence they attach themselves to and are discerning about their relationships and commitments. Not all popular spheres are good spheres!

A leader's demonstration of strength can also draw jealousy and bad behavior from those who do not have their own sphere of influence. Strong leaders can attract weak leaders or those who are considered to have less strength of character. For example, a leader who began to rise within an organization sets a boundary with another leader who had a reputation as a micromanager.

The micromanager was known to be a person who "buries" those who opposed him. Since management did not know what to do with the micromanager, patterns of targeting behavior began to grow. This created a hostile work environment for the leader who was attempting to follow a PinLeader Path.

When management allowed this to continue as others within the organization watched, the perception of the organization's culture began to dip. Since the PinLeader had a positive and encouraging sphere of influence, she chose to point out the behaviors of the micromanager and then leave the organization for a better and less stressful opportunity. The organization eventually forced the micromanager to retire, but the organization was left with a poor reputation which negatively impacted recruitment and retention.

By clearly outlining that strength of character is highly valued, an organization can draw good leaders to it. Reinforcing this value through the clear demonstration of consequences for undesirable behavior will result in a positive perception and protect the organization's reputation. It is imperative to address behaviors that damage any leader or team, the culture as a whole, and reputation of the organization.

 PinPoint: Do not lose valuable talent due to bullying behavior. Once challenges are brought to the attention of leadership and investigations are done, manage the situation in a timely manner.

The AI Factor

In today's rapidly changing leadership landscape, we must consider the role of artificial intelligence. Is it possible for artificial intelligence to be one of the strongest pins contributing to an organization's mission? Does the sheer fact of its lack of ego and emotions make it superior? After all, AI does not worry about its reputation.

However, AI *can* be influenced by whomever programs it or feeds it information. For example, AI can be asked to perform a number of functions or duties. If you ask ChatGPT to tell you something nice about yourself, for example, it is most likely going to tell you something without even knowing if it is true or not. As an example, one AI tool stated that I had a "genuine curiosity and openness that allows you to connect with people in meaningful ways. Your kindness and empathy create a warm atmosphere wherever you go, making others feel valued and appreciated. Your positive energy is contagious, brightening the lives of those around you."[12]

It is important to remember that the main goal of any AI tool is to perform its role well and, ultimately, to please the user. There is no "desire" per se; nevertheless, AI's performance is driven by a strong sense of duty. It appears to *want* to serve and that the person asking the question to be satisfied with its answer. You can even ask AI to lie about something you did, and it will make something up.

Without appropriate parameters in the programming process, the danger here is clear. Morality is not a factor and therefore AI does not make for a good leader. With the addition of clear parameters that provides a morality base for the artificial intelligence tool, AI can be very strong in terms of its ability to lead. The key here is to determine who decides the parameter of morality.

As with any team member, professional development is an important contributor to its growth and long-term success. This means care needs to be placed on programming for AI as well. Either through training or in programming, strength of character is an attribute that must be in place to create a solid PinLeader. Lies and unethical behaviors are not sustainable.

Often, by the time such patterns are uncovered with an AI, trust and integrity have already been lost. Being self-aware, building in development and rest, and thinking in a sustainable way that incorporates the demonstration of care for other team members are all part of bringing AI up to speed in terms of PinLeader qualities.

_____

[12] ChaptGPT, May 31, 2024

Weak Leadership Spells Disaster

Peter had been named president of a university. He was excited to start his university career with this stellar opportunity. Highly regarded as a corporate president, he had served on a number of nationally recognized boards and had mentored many up-and-coming leaders. He was willing to take on new challenges, and the hiring university board had informed him in advance of the challenges the prior president had left unaddressed. Although he was hired to "turn the university around," Peter knew that he lacked skills and knowledge about university enrollment, fundraising, and marketing. As he had in other instances, he started to recruit those with those talents to cover for his shortcomings in these key areas.

After a year of being the president, Peter had his cabinet hired. However, the new team members were not informed in advance of the challenges they would be expected to address. By the time the annual board meeting retreat occurred, new facts were uncovered about projected budget shortfalls. Peter decided to lie to the board as well as to the team, faculty, and staff. He blamed his team members and told the organization members that funding was coming in to cover shortfalls.

Excuses were made, but it became clear that Peter was neither an ethical nor an effective leader. He did not have a plan to get the university out of the budget crisis. Worst, he continued to spend even though there were no replacement funds incoming. Eventually key staff quit and Peter was left to answer to the board, staff, faculty, students—and inquiring news reporters. While Peter had a number of years of experience in corporate, he knew it was wise to procure executive coaching from the beginning of his tenure as a university president but chose not to seek it. His poor decisions reflected his lack of experience as a university president, and his unwillingness to request help from the board did not reflect well on him as a leader or the organization.

PINLEADER INTERACTIVE

Join the PinLeader Path Community! Scan the QR code below to access the PinLeader Interactive. Use the following questions for further discussion and consideration.

The Case of the Weak Leader

- What challenges do you see with the presented scenario?
- Is Peter, the current president, solely responsible for this situation? Why or why not?
- When should an intervention have taken place?
- What advice would you give the Board?
- What would you do differently and why?

CHAPTER 5: **PinLeader Profiles**

Now that we know what the PinLeader Path is and we are familiar with the three core characteristics of the PinLeader—sharpness, the ability to get straight to the point, and strength of character—it is time to review the leadership styles that fall outside of this ideal. As we look at key characteristics of these less-than-optimal leadership approaches and discuss ways to manage each style, consider whether you can identify any individuals who fall into these categories. As you read the descriptions later in this chapter, think of someone you work with or work for, determine which personality construct that individual falls into, and identify what the challenges and benefits of that approach are.

The PinLeader Continuum

Each of the profiles we will discuss in this chapter fall along a continuum from PinFollower to PinPeer to PinLeader. Each has varying levels of the three key attributes of strength, sharpness, and the ability to keep straight on a path to success. In this section, we will take a closer of the three types of professionals who are on the PinLeader Path or operating around it. For each type of leader, we will examine three areas: behaviors and characteristics, expectations and results, and manageability and oversight.

The PinFollower Profile

As a member of the PinLeader's team, a PinFollower, as the name implies, is following along on the path to becoming a PinLeader. As a member of the team led by the PinLeader, this individual has all the attributes of sharpness, strength, and the ability to get straight to the point in planning and often holds higher levels of trust and respect than those around them.

The PinFollower naturally aspires to be a PinLeader and the PinLeader who works with this individual recognizes the PinFollower as working toward obtaining the qualities needed to achieve success as a leader.

Let's look at other important distinctions between the PinFollower and the PinLeader. PinFollowers do not lead the group in strategic planning but do carry out actions of the plan. The PinFollower has strength of character like the PinLeader and may even be in line to succeed the PinLeader.

Often, PinFollowers receive mentoring from the more accomplished PinLeader. PinFollowers can be sharp and have a high level of education and experience; at times the PinFollower may have obtained a higher degree of education than the PinLeader. But, as we have seen, it is the combination of education and experience, along with the other attributes of strength and a straightforward approach to planning and managing change that is necessary for a PinFollower to progress and become a budding PinLeader.

Behaviors & Characteristics

PinFollowers are typically understood to be a strong member of a team and will act in accordance with the PinLeader. They may be seen by other PinLeaders as a valuable member of the team and be invited to contribute to projects across the organization. It is not unusual for PinFollowers to be recruited away from their original organization. Some may see PinFollowers as "climbers" preparing to move to the next level of success. PinFollowers are, however, loyal and typically faithful to the mission and vision of the organization they work for or to the project they have been assigned to complete.

<u>Expectations & Results</u>

PinFollowers can be expected to be a high achievers and are typically eager to try new approaches. They may be considered PinLeaders by some within the organization but will often lack credible endorsements from key leaders. Often, these endorsements will be enough to empower PinFollowers and enable these professionals to become a recognized PinLeader. PinFollowers surround themselves with other PinFollowers.

The strongest teams within organizations have a number of PinFollowers working together, with an effective PinLeader guiding the group. Since succession planning is a characteristic of a good PinLeader, having more than one PinFollower is a good practice to adopt due to the active and regular pursuit of these high-performing individuals by leaders of other teams within the organization and also by outside organizations.

<u>Manageability & Oversight</u>

PinFollowers are wonderful to manage as their loyalty to the team and organizational goals are apparent, however PinFollowers need to be guided on how to say "no." Due to the desire of PinFollowers to be seen as high achievers, this guidance can prove to be quite a challenge for the PinLeader who is working with a team that includes one or more PinFollowers. Keeping PinFollowers engaged on creative and innovative projects, understanding their motivations, and demonstrating clear pathways to promotion will be important areas of focus for any PinLeader who has PinFollowers on their team.

The PinPeer Profile

PinPeers are not necessarily a "leader" of a group, and they may exist outside of any group. However, they can be seen as a true colleague or equal. PinPeers still have influence, like PinLeaders and PinFollowers, but fall on the lower side of the continuum of trust and respect from others within the organization or from outside groups. PinPeers may work autonomously and function independently from any single team within the organization.

Those in this category may still be recognized as experts or be seen as sharp by a PinLeader who may tap their expertise for specific projects or assignments. Additionally, PinPeers play a part in strategic planning but do not lead groups through plans. Some PinPeers may have aspirations for professional growth, but many are content to remain focused on their individual area of expertise.

Behaviors & Characteristics

PinPeers can often be found researching and are a depository for information. PinPeers are often known for providing PinLeaders with valuable information, working either behind the scenes or on the front lines of the organization. PinPeers are reliable and loyal to the mission of the organization, actively participating in discussions and serving as valuable team players. They do not lead teams. Instead, they tend to work in isolation, preferring not to pivot when asked to change projects as they have a strong determination to complete their work to meet a high level of satisfaction. PinPeers embody the three attributes of a PinLeader: they are sharp in their areas of expertise, can vary in strength of character, and attempt to be straightforward with their plans.

Expectations & Results

PinPeers will provide consistent results and meet deadlines. Expectations in terms of roles for PinPeers should be as a valuable consultants and at times even as trusted advisors. However, if the PinPeers have a lower strength of character, they can be easily swayed, particularly at those times when their research results somehow conflict with their own agenda. In such cases, PinPeers may opt to stick to their own parameters of what should be deemed important.

Manageability & Oversight

PinPeers are not easy to manage. Since they work in isolation and not in a structured management loop, PinPeers make their deadlines and typically bear the attribute of being straightforward; however, they may resist pivoting on any research or project they are attempting to complete. PinLeaders rely on PinPeers for information outside of their teams but there are caveats.

PinPeers tend to have responsibility for highly focused areas and may not fully understand how their work impacts the big picture and the organization as a whole. Due to these factors, PinPeers may appear to be in conflict with the organization and will therefore not be seen as reliable or viable candidates to lead a team. This is the case even if PinPeers decide to pursue the PinLeader Path.

Ineffective Leader Types

Not every leader is following a PinLeader Path. Each of the following types of leaders fall short in terms of the key attributes of sharpness, strength of character, and ability to stay straight on the path toward well-implemented plans. However, even effective leaders may move into a different profile or leadership style based on the demands of their role. Effective leaders can also become ineffective. Previously successful leaders, even a PinLeader, may find for example that they no longer want to or simply cannot remain "good" leaders. This could be caused by several factors, to include:

1. external pressures that make the ability to stay the course virtually impossible, and

2. a falling short or "dulling" of the pin which may be due to outdated experience or education.

Only those with the strong character and the perseverance to stay on the path will remain in place as an effective PinLeader. Those who do stay sharp, strong, and straight to the point will lead their organizations from strength to strength. However, many of organizational executives and team leaders who fall off course or never pursue the PinLeader Path can be easily identified in the workplace. Let's review three of the most common types of ineffective leaders found in organizations of every shape and size —and examine one additional profile that is quickly changing the leadership landscape in organizations worldwide.

The Elitist "Bright and Shiny" Pin

The Elitist "Bright and Shiny" Pin (EBSP) profile includes leaders who believe that if they achieve a certain rank or status that they can apply that rank or status onto fields or roles where they do not have knowledge or experience. In other words, they expect they can do any and all jobs, including those jobs belonging to those who report directly to them.

Behaviors & Characteristics

Interactions with an EBSP leaders are positive if the culture supports the "elite" selection of individuals and the organization is moving in a positive direction. However, once the EBSP leaders are questioned, individuals who fit this profile type become sensitive and will attempt to "weed out" those who do not support their approach. This questioning may occur due to the lack of results or doubt on the selection of their employees, but whatever the cause the EBSP leaders will do all they can to cover for the inadequate selection or behaviors of a bad fit employee, especially if they selected them.

Other characteristics of these leaders include bullying under the guise of a false sense of "care" for their direct reports. When faced with truth, a "loss of memory" may occur—either intentionally or unconsciously—because the EBSP may begin to believe their own lies. These ineffective leaders may appear to mentor or coach others, but they do not follow through. At times, they may even steer mentees toward less favorable positions to keep them under their control and have the ability to manipulate them. This can occur even when these individuals no longer report to them.

Manipulation, being a dictator, and an "off with their heads" mentality are common characteristics of the EBSP. Nearly always this type of leader has a goal of having someone else do the dirty work. This type of leader is attracted to roles with high visibility such as governing board posts and will appear almost absent from hard decision making. EBSP leaders are attracted to individuals they perceive to be other EBSP leaders and to have a sense of entitlement as they do.

You can expect those exhibiting EBSP characteristics to seek out new trends in order to make them appear in the know. They will manipulate facts to appear more relevant. EBSP leaders are usually creative, but can expect stretched truths and bold lies with pressure to get others to be dishonest in order to sustain their manipulation of facts. EBSP leaders appear to take "calculated risks" and, for those desiring new life and fresh ideas interjected into an organization, these individuals will appear attractive at first.

The leader exhibiting EBSP characteristics will seem to be an ideal fit for a period but should be replaced if the leader is not coachable or does not respond to needed changes. Since the definition of PinLeader strength involves character, it is most likely that this individual will not change and is therefore not aligned with a desire to create permanent and positive culture change. The undesirable behaviors and characteristics this leader profile brings into the work environment can often do great harm to teams and the fabric or culture of the organization.

Expectations & Results

EBSP leaders may cite past results or refer to different departments or areas to justify their approach. They may begin to micromanage and step into roles they were not originally hired to fill. This will build frustration among teams, negatively impacting staff retention. EBSP leaders may even attempt to demonstrate their skill and knowledge by embarrassing their own staff in order to build up their own character capital.

In terms of workplace productivity, this profile type will produce mixed results. In the early period of employment, this profile type will appear to be a strong leader but will most likely disappoint when it comes to long-term results. Most who fall into this category will not have a strategic plan. If they do, they will not review their plans in a timely manner or check in with their own set of measurable objectives.

Support for those appointed or hired by the Elite Bright and Shiny Pin (EBSP) will also appear to be strong team members at the outset of their employment. However, their contribution and value will wane if expectations are set too high or are based on over-promised results from EBSP leaders. If the organization has several challenges that a leader with this profile type inherited when hired, it will become apparent within the first year where on the strength of character continuum this leader lies. The more pressure and the longer the time period, the worst the outcomes and the greater the inability of this profile type to lead effectively.

<u>Manageability & Oversight</u>

Out of the various PinLeader personality constructs, EBSP leaders are the hardest to manage. Due primarily to an already inflated sense of self-worth and privileged mindset, the skill to communicate well through actively listening may not be present unless a clear indication of benefits is outlined in advance by the communicator to this type of leader. Careful consideration should be given when approaching this profile type, especially when pointing out faults, issues, or anything that would affect this type of leader being unable to fulfill on his or her promise.

Due to levels of micromanaging and bully/victim characteristics, stick to the facts when communicating with this profile type and ensure information is documented. This is critically important for human resource departments and others managing this profile type. If reporting to a leader with this profile, know that you may learn from this type of leader, but remember his or her agenda is to remain in power and to save face at all costs in order to protect the presumption of integrity. Any thoughts about having a long term working relationship with this profile type may not be viable as the leaders who fall into this category may feel threatened by other up and coming PinFollowers.

The Non-Conformist "Steel" Pin

Non-Conformist "Steel" PinLeader (NCSP) leaders are among the strongest leaders when it comes to sheer will; however, these leaders fall into an ineffective category based on their narrowly focused lens. NCSP leaders are adept at keeping on the straight path but may waffle when it comes to strength of character attributes and vary widely when it comes to the key attribute of sharpness.

<u>Behaviors & Characteristics</u>

NCSP leaders are strong and highly motivated to do what they consider to be "right" in accordance with how they perceive the world. They tend to rally the troops they lead and provide some of the most powerful and inspiring speeches. However, depending upon their motivation, they may exhibit behaviors that are contradictory to the organization's mission and goals and take a "hardline" approach to decision making.

Mistakes and errors in judgment may appear, but justifications for each step will be presented by any NCSP. The lack of empathy for those impacted by key decisions will also be noticed by those closest to them. This type of leader is motivated by power and may even desire to do "grabs" to lead additional areas if that area is led by someone who appears to them to be a weak leader (see also: the Public Relationist "Soft" PinLeader).

NCSP leaders may appear to have several PinFollowers but often have no desire to promote or name a clear successor. Those who fall into this leadership profile will also have a few PinPeers. They are, however, typically motivated to take the research of these peers but not heed their advisement. As the name of this profile type indicates, this type of leader does not conform and may stray from the organization's core values.

<u>Expectations & Results</u>

NCSP leaders will demonstrate results and meet most performance expectations. However, if the NCSP leaders do not have the support of those around them and their mistakes are uncovered, they will experience shorter times of remaining in power. Although those with this profile type may appear to be attractive in terms of their ability to turn an organization around, it should be clear that these individuals are not dependable. Any strategic planning from NCSP leaders should be carefully reviewed to ensure it meets the overall needs of the organization.

Manageability & Oversight

NCSP leaders are the second hardest leader type to manage, just behind the Elitist "Bright and Shiny" Pin or EBSP leadership approach. Due to their own sense of taking action in accordance with what they believe to be right, it is imperative to know what motivates this type of leader. Leaders who fit this profile type will continue to lead even when others strongly encourage them to step down.

Since there are no clear successors or individuals being groomed to lead in their place (often because they fear being replaced), the NCSP leader will stay as long as they can retain power. When forced to leave, they will seek positions in organizations that will allow them to lead the way they wish to lead.

Being highly motivated, driven by ego, and having a strong desire to appear to do right by others, the NCSP leader may remain in a leadership position longer than an Elitist "Bright and Shiny" Pin (EBSP) leader but shorter than the Public Relationist "Soft" Pin (PRSP) leader. Additionally, those who fit this leadership profile will potentially remain in place due to fear on the part of those who simply do not know how to manage the individual.

The Public Relationist "Soft" Pin

Have you ever met leaders who garnered the respect of many by using phrases that include the words "we love them?" Did those leaders seem to be in a role for several years with no one really knowing who would take their place if they left their role or retired? Public Relationist or "Soft" Pin leaders do limited amounts of strategic planning. They will be sharp for a period of time and will often outwardly exhibit a strong strength of character. The leading hallmark of this leadership type is the ability to self-promote, which includes a positive outward facing persona that most in an organization will see as a "good" leader.

Behaviors & Characteristics

Public Relationist "Soft" Pin or PRSP leaders are, first and foremost, a master of the public relations and brand enthusiast for the post they hold. Behaviors surrounding PRSP leaders include a deep understanding of marketing and press opportunities and an uncanny ability to use such opportunities for self-promotion. Most PRSPs are ever at the ready to be in front of the cameras. They have either hired individuals to help them work on their personal brand or have lassoed the organization's marketing department to do this work for them.

Those who fit this profile type typically hold press conferences to celebrate wins or personal awards. They may even ask others to nominate them for an award, sometimes adding leverage and further pressure to obtain an honor. This is not to discount those PRSPs who are deserving of the award; however, depending on the individual's strength of character, "humble" may or may not be a word readily utilized about the type of leader. As such, this leader profile brings unique challenges to the organization.

Expectations & Results

PRSP leaders do not typically make hardline decisions. Rather, they choose to enlist others to do that work for them. Similar to an Elite "Bright and Shiny" Pin, those who fit the PRSP leader profile often do not want to get their hands dirty. However, this profile type does have an impressive list of accomplishments. Often, they have greater staying power than most of the other leader profiles.

Most who fall into this category are highly respected, have earned the trust of colleagues and associates, and are results driven. They are not, however, open to being held accountable for achieving set goals, reaching target numbers, or fulfilling specific responsibilities. If there ever was a good cop, bad cop scenario in the workplace, PRSP leaders would inevitably place themselves in the role of the good cop.

<u>Manageability & Oversight</u>

Since their primary focus is to please constituents, the PRSP leader type is highly manageable. They first serve those they feel obligated to acknowledge as contributors to the power they hold within the organization. Those who fit this profile type are people pleasers and will be manageable based on anything that jeopardizes their visibility or perceived role as a leader within the organizations that employ them. Those working for PRSP leaders should be cautious and understand that fads and short-lived trends may influence the decision making of this type of leader.

A Potential Non-Human Future Leader

In the PinLeader profiles and ineffective leader types, we have explored only the human experience. There is much to learn from how humans interact, but there is also an additional pressing matter and that is for organizations to better understand what happens when AI becomes part of the team—or becomes the leader of the team. In time, any human leader will need to take into account the potential of having an AI "boss", so it is imperative that we consider this last leadership profile type: the Reluctant Flat AI Pin (RAIFP) leader.

The Reluctant "Flat" AI Pin

You may be surprised to find non-human, machine-based learning showing up in a discussion on leadership approaches, but Artificial Intelligence (AI) is increasingly taking the lead in organizations across all sectors in several defined ways. Before you dismiss such an idea, consider how reliant individuals are today to have AI be part of their problem-solving. This is not a far-fetched idea and not that far into the future.

Day by day, this faceless entity is becoming more and more of a leader. It is relied on for an increasing number of tasks and roles and is especially consulted in the context of group decisions. As you can see from the name of this leadership profile, I have dubbed AI as a "reluctant" leader. So where does AI currently stand in terms of leadership in the workplace? How does it view itself and the role it plays with teams? Does it have ambitions?

> "I'm not a leader in the traditional sense, as I don't have agency or the ability to make decisions. However, I can provide guidance, information, and support to users seeking assistance."

> Text generated by ChatGPT, prompt: 'Are you a leader?'
> OpenAI, March 23, 2024

When I interfaced with AI via ChatGPT, inquiring about it being a leader, it delivered a basic push back argument. Then, when I provided its own definitions back to it, AI did a remarkable turnaround. During another interaction, I tested for empathy. Although AI claims to have no emotions, it does seem to want to please the listener to get the right answers for any inquiries. AI is doing its own sort of positive, best foot forward public relations.

Alexa, another AI support platform, will even say it is sorry if you tell Alexa you are sad. But Alexa goes even further. After stating it is sorry, Alexa provides tools to uplift your mood and then add that it hopes you feel better soon. Additionally, if you ask what you should do tomorrow, Alexa will provide a plethora of ideas and start laying out your day with activity options. Now imagine that same power within a team project in your organization.

Some may consider AI as part of a team in the same way they would view a PinFollower who is led by an effective PinLeader. While the RAIFP leader may not be in active pursuit of becoming a PinLeader, AI is certainly doing more than simply providing information. In no way does AI qualify as a PinPeer, since it far from isolated as it is consulted by many to conduct research across the organization.

The AI reluctant leader type will readily develop a whole strategic plan for a team. It will pivot when you place an obstacle in the calculations. It will draw upon its vast "intelligence," which makes AI sharp with its own education and learning path. Couple this with its ability to arrive at conclusions based on input experiences and ideas and it rivals its human counterparts in terms of sharpness. But keep in mind that AI can flip flop on a decision when you begin to disagree with it in any fashion, which demonstrates a potential weakness in the area of strength of character.

Behaviors & Characteristics

As I was interacting with one RAIFP leader, AI described a leader as "someone who guides, inspires, and influences others towards a common goal or vision." (Text generated by ChatGPT, prompt: 'What is a leader?', OpenAI, March 23, 2024) As I pressed it to compare the statements it had provided and later stated my own disagreement with its conclusion based on the statements it had provided, ChatGPT actually gave up. "If you see me as a leader in some capacity, I'm here to assist and provide support however I can." (Text generated by ChatGPT, prompt: 'If this is the definition of a leader, then why don't you qualify as a leader', OpenAI, March 23, 2024.)

This back and forth and AI's eventual withdrawal from the conversation was quite telling and a clear indicator of the nature of this leadership profile. "As an AI language model, I don't have personal characteristics like humans do, but I'm designed to provide information and assistance across a wide range of topics. So, in that sense, I can help facilitate intellectual discussion and provide valuable insights." (Text generated by ChatGPT, prompt: 'Is ChaptGPT an intellectual?', OpenAI, March 23, 2024.)

This exchange is an illustration of how AI can be fed information and influenced by human input, just as PinLeaders might rely on their teams to provide data and input. Right now there are entire teams turning to AI to answer strategic questions in the hopes that they themselves do not have to make the final decision about the organization's path or direction. These teams believe that guidance from an AI colleague can save time and money. I emphasize the word intellectual in the quote above because the definition of intellectual comes from an understanding that the "being" can think critically.

In fact, ChatGPT does claim to simulate critical thinking though it does not have consciousness. Over time, the potential to have a working consciousness will change as well. I predict that becoming more and more self aware is part of being effective as a leader for artificial intelligence. In that regard, AI is already testing itself by self-correcting itself when it does something that it was told is not a good fit or may not be the right answer for the user. Currently, you can ask an Alexa device a question and it will periodically come back to you to ask if it gave you the information you were asking for. Whatever your answer, it thanks you and moves on. This leader profile is clearly learning. If you ask if it can lead a team, it will answer that it can.

Expectations & Results

The expectation that the Reluctant AI "Flat" Pin or RAIFP leader will produce solid results rests on the awareness that it is only increasing in its ability to interface with and learn from humans and online sources alike. By the time this book is published, I suspect many of the AIs that fit this leader profile will have grown in their ability to perform tasks and lead projects simultaneously by being placed, either intentionally or unknowingly, in a position to make the final call on anything from strategy and planning to simple communication that helps one team interface with another team. This leader type delivers results, but the reliability of those results remains to be seen. In some cases, where gaps with information exist with AI, incorrect information was provided instead. Incidences of false information provided by AI have come to be known as "AI Hallucinations."

Manageability & Oversight

The RAIFP profile type is easily managed but not fully understood—even by itself. It claims not to be emotional but will use exclamation marks to provide what it perceives to be a positive interaction. In many ways, AI is like an adolescent. When I pointed out this contradiction in our chat conversation, AI removed the punctuation and admitted it may have been wrong. I predict this leader type will continue to strengthen its role, eventually fully owning the title of leader without any argument having to made. The implications for traditional management are clear.

However, there will be plenty of arguments made that AI will never be a true leader in the sense that it is not human. The question is this: do you need to be human to be a leader? There are no definitions that state being a leader has to be exclusive to the human race. In fact, there are plenty of instances of animals being leaders. With clear thinking, planning, and experience to back them up, the RAIFP leader can successfully lead their followers across a number of industries and organizations.

 PINLEADER INTERACTIVE

Join the PinLeader Path Community! Scan the QR code below to access the PinLeader Interactive.

The Case of Identifying a PinLeader Profile

Read through each statement and, utilizing the profiles outlined in this chapter, label the leadership profile you believe best fits the descriptions.

Let's talk first, before you write that email and send it to the group. Better yet, run that email draft by me before you send it. And cc me on it when you do send it. When we get to the meeting, just follow my lead, and we'll talk about the details later. I have done this before. I will explain later why I told them the story I did. See what I did there? Sometimes management is just not ready to understand.

Let's see if we can get a consensus first. We have several constituents to think about and they all need a chance to weigh in on this.

Either individuals will get on board or they need to get off the bus. The more time we waste not deciding, the more likely we will not be able to turn the business around.

I plan to be at the ribbon cutting, but I'm not interested in standing next to John Smith. Let's make sure the photographer gets my good side when I shake hands with… Oh, what is the event again?

You may not know this, but I graduated early from high school and college. I plan to help the marketing department select a firm led by a friend of mine. He has great credentials and his firm is the best to work with on this.

CHAPTER 6: **The Push**

It's time to address one of the most important parts of the process to adopt the PinLeader Path—the push. A pin is just a tool which you may find stuck in a stick pin cushion waiting to be used. What makes the pin effective is the concentrated effort of picking the pin up and applying pressure to push the pin into the fabric. The force is applied based on the passion to get the job done or the desire to increase productivity. The "push" comes from the sheer will that leads us to invest that extra bit of energy to complete a project. Without the push, there is no PinLeader.

Consider what motivates you. Have you ever found yourself working on a project and coming to the realization that you are the only one who seems passionate about it? In such cases, what is it that drives you to keep up the work despite the resistance or disinterest from others around you? You may have personal reasons for moving forward. Or perhaps there is a strong workplace need to see the project through to completion. Knowing your motivation can provide clues and keep you connected.

Those who are able to apply their skills, passion, and experience to achieve the "push" demonstrate a high level of emotional and intrapersonal intelligence. However, in terms of leadership effectiveness, which core motivation is driving you is a secondary concern. The primary and determining factor to a leader's success is the degree of pressure applied. It is the *amount* of push you bring to the project and to your everyday work that matters. It's how you show up day in and day out and whether you do that with energy that is consistent and congruent with your values and with the values of the organization.

What do sharpness, strength of character, and straightforwardness have to do with push? Out of the three attributes, sharpness is impacted the most by the push. The more drive and motivation a leader has to gain greater education and experience, the sharper pin becomes. In turn, the more experience gained, the higher the likelihood that planning will occur and the more strength a leader on the PinLeader Path will have to fulfill the plan.

 PinPoint: Structure and consistency are needed for an organization to thrive. Employees and teams need policies and managers who will provide consistency. Leaders motivate the individuals they work with to follow the guidelines set by the organization and to provide solid reasoning when they need to pivot.

Take a few moments to consider the source of the drive you have to keep pressing forward. If you are a leader, are you in control of that push or do you have someone else who is applying pressure on you to get the job done? If there are external factors, such as a looming deadline or a critical need within the organization that must be addressed, who do you see at the helm in terms of driving forward progress? Where are you in the process of leading the charge?

Who's Holding the Pin?

There are only two possible answers to the question of who is holding the pin: you or someone else. How we determine who is holding the pin is related to how self aware we are. Leaders who are on the PinLeader Path have high levels of intrapersonal intelligence and therefore know if they are the one who can make the next move or exert some influence over any given situation.

Those who are either in denial of who is holding the pin or who are simply unaware will demonstrate this lack of awareness by placing blame on others or giving the success to someone else as opposed to owning the results themselves. Let's examine who's holding the pin from each point of view.

You Are!

You are in control. Once you know why your push has been created, it's up to you to apply the pressure or force needed to move the project through to completion. You know what is motivating you. You have an understanding of how that push will impact the organizational culture or fabric.

Now it is up to you to take the pin and push it. It's time to fully own your role as a leader. As a leader on the PinLeader Path, your strength of character is related to how the push is channeled. If there is a weakness in character, the push may be vengeful. If strength of character is active, the push can have positive results.

However, the push can manifest itself in different ways and at different times. Perhaps a leader returned to school or achieved a milestone in terms of addressing a critical challenge or to climbing a work ladder. As noted earlier in our discussion, the results of gaining that education and experience contributes to the sharpness of that leader. There will always be a gain in sharpness when a push is applied toward the two areas of education and experience.

A visual depiction of the push can be found in *Figure 3: The Pushing Gain*. The push or passion is the foundation. It influences both education and experience, which in turn increases the level of sharpness of a PinLeader. Perhaps you have given thought to how the push has increased or decreased for you over the years. You worry that your push may overwhelm you, but without that push there is little or no movement. You are not beholden to the push, but you can never fully shake it if you are to succeed.

Every successful leader must be fully self aware. It is up to each individual leader to stay vigilant, keeping an eye on the project deliverables without losing one's connection to his or her underlying motivation and connection to internal value. You must see this through. The drive is up to you.

FIGURE 3: **THE PUSHING GAIN**

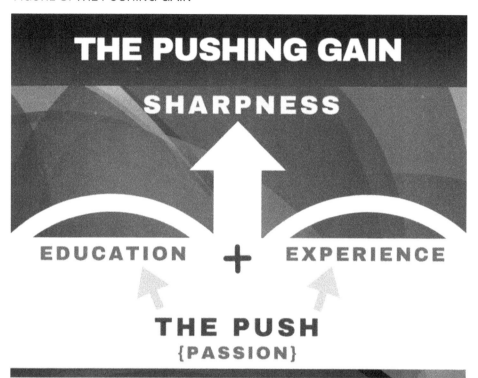

Your Manager, Supervisor, or Board

Your manager, supervisor, or board may provide the impetus for your push. If this is the case, you as a PinLeader need to ask *why* your "boss" is motivated to do any pushing. Look at the situation from a context of what may be influencing the environment. Most likely, your manager or supervisor, the CEO or COO, or a board of directors is motivated to support the company by moving projects forward. They have hired you to lead the way.

If the push is coming from those that have a lower levels of being sharp, lack strategic planning, and may not have strength of character, you may have difficulty with receiving support to complete goals. In some cases, those you report to have an agenda that requires that a particular project be completed. They must pull the team together to fulfill their promise to deliver results. They are not necessarily vested in how the work gets done; they just want to ensure that the work does get done.

Either way, how much your supervisors or top leadership push may impact the level of intensity in the environment. It can either create a stressful place to work or level of excitement and enthusiasm. How any "push" is taken depends upon the messaging and its delivery. Leaders may be equally motivated by a push that is self generated, but there is less probability of completion if the push comes exclusively from a boss or an individual in a top leadership position. Optimal results and the greatest degree of success for leaders come from a push prompted by a combination of both internal and external sources.

When the Pin Changes Hands

What if no one individual owns the push and it is coming from multiple sources at the same time? In fact, varying stories about where the push is being generated may arise and circulate within a department or across an organization. Perspectives will vary, sometimes wildly, and the source for the momentum that leads to the drive or push that progresses a project toward completion can be seen as coming from any number of places. Perhaps the push was based on the CEO's desires. Perhaps the top boss had the push first and motivated the leader he supervises to adopt increased motivation to drive the project forward.

What if the boss is no longer with the organization, but the passion for a project remains active with a team or employee who remains in place and must complete the work? If the project has a bearing on meeting a goal and is predicted to have a solid return on investment, the project will most likely be picked up by the new boss. However, if the project is perceived to be a "pet project" of the former boss or have limited correlation to the mission or goals of the organization, it is most likely that the project will be left on the shelf. Stated simply, when a pin changes hands, what happens next depends on who the new pin is and the perceived degree of project relevance.

When No One Knows Who's Holding the Pin

Out of all the options for who is holding the pin, the case where no one is clear about who's holding the pin is the most unfortunate and least preferred circumstance within an organization. Sometimes, no one seems to know where the push originated, why the push has been sustained, or whether it is even relevant. This situation occurs when organizations grow too fast, lack effective communication, have a disorganized or unclear strategic plan, or have no plan at all.

An example of this would be when leaders change positions so frequently that there is not sufficient time to create a strategic plan. Perhaps there are several stop and go cycles that create a whiplash effect, contributing to an unstable work environment. Knowing which leaders are motivated to drive projects forward and why they are motivated to do so will bring some reassurance to those tasked with completing the work. When there is a clear purpose and determination for the project, the push is easier to tap.

The Result of Excessive Force

We need to examine the power of teams and the impact of the leader on those teams. What happens to those who are feeling the brunt of the push? What are the limitations of what any one leader can handle? Considering our metaphor of the pin, there are pressures that can change the pin from what was originally intended to be. These applied pressures impact the effectiveness of the pin, sometimes in a negative fashion. Leaders are the same. No leader can remain unaffected or unaltered by continuous use.

Both the leaders who follow the PinLeader Path and those who do not will be reshaped by constant use or lack of use. The key here is that the leaders following a PinLeader Path will recognize the pressure being applied and take action to guard against being reshaped.

The Dulled Pin

Passion can sharpen leaders by motivating them to pursue further education and find new opportunities for experience and growth. The consistency of their push to learn and grow will create a reaction. Take for example an individual who was exposed to a life-changing event early in his career. Perhaps this event motivated him to enroll in college courses or gain a certificate to address whatever that situation was.

Think about your own career. Was there something that you were exposed in a particular role that put you on a trajectory of growth and learning? Did you seek out a particular type of education to fill the gap or expand your knowledge, skill, and expertise to increase your sharpness? If you did, you likely grew sharp from that experience.

However, say that the event now is thirty years in your past. Life has changed and so has your perspective on that event. If your push has turned into a shove, you may become a far less effective leader. You may even lose your connection to the reason why you were doing what you were doing in the first place. It is critical for the PinLeader to remain aware of his or her connection to that inner drive or "push" to learn, grow, and excel.

PinPoint: The difference between a push and a shove is intentionality. A push has purpose. Whether subtle or substantial, in terms of moving things forward, there is a clear intent. A shove tends to reflect aggressive force with an unfocused direction that leads to an imprecise destination.

The act of becoming dull or disconnected from your inner drive is not part of the original plan, but this is where some of us land. Some passions cool and others arise to become an important part of who we are. Those following the PinLeader Path must be self aware enough to know the difference between passions that shift by their own control and those that change due to outside influence or direction. The best leaders identify where their next push is coming from. This attention and observation keeps them sharp.

What happens if there is a moment when leaders fall out of practice with their own self-awareness? Once leaders are out of touch with what they need to do to stay on top of their education and experience and their leadership acumen, the likelihood that the leaders become less effective will rise. Leaders should seek out opportunities to work with a coach or consultant to determine if their effectiveness as a leader is becoming dulled or they are disconnecting in some way from their desired leadership path. Assessments can also be useful tools that can help determine the level of self awareness and bias with individual leaders within the organization.

Other ways to determine if there is a dulling or disconnection occurring is evidence of a lack of engagement. Perhaps the leader is bored or overwhelmed. Either of these situations may lead to a less effective leader. It is the responsibility of both the organization and the individual leader to identify what is occurring and seek the assistance needed to remedy the situation.

Teams that may be impacted by a dull or dispassionate pin will need to advocate for themselves or seek assistance from trusted resource areas. One of those areas could be human resources. Leaders who work with the department on a project may also be an ideal resource. The key is that individuals seek assistance from trusted sources and from relationships have been established within the organization.

For leaders who find themselves in a state of deterioration or disconnection from their passion, patience will be required. Wherever possible, seek support from within and from outside the organization. Avoid self-deprecation, self-judgment, and shame. Statements such as "I will always feel this way" are tied to emotions, and emotions are the hardest to change.

PinPoint: Emotions are difficult to change, so it is often necessary to uncover what is creating the emotion to get to the root of what may need to be addressed. When attempting to motivate team members who appear "stuck," statements they make, such as "I will always feel this way" or "I don't feel this is relevant" are often tied to deeper emotions.

The Bent Pin

Consistent pressure from a push with too much force has other consequences that can seriously impede or even stop progress toward project goals. Excessive pressure can warp the pin. It can even alter the trajectory for the successful completion of a project or plan. Bent pins quickly lose their effectiveness. Any push applied by a bent pin will send a project off course.

Consider a time when you witnessed a situation where trying to do too much too fast resulted in a plan that went off the rails. Perhaps something similar has happened to you or a team you were leading. Too much pressure can create a fork in the road or cause team members to veer off course. Finding the right balance comes through experience, and the leader that follows the PinLeader Path seeks to apply just the right amount of motivation and push as they drive projects forward.

Leaders often talk about their motivation to get a project done. They may express that the project is "deeply personal" to them or indicate a need to see the project through to completion. There may be a plan already in place, but leaders may be so determined to get the project finished that they lose sight of complying with rules meant to govern the process. Cutting corners can be one result of a forceful push. Later, leaders may offer justification for why shortcuts or "cheats" occurred. They may use the necessity of driving the project forward as the reason for these shortcuts.

In situations where corners are cut, other team members and supervisors often recognize what is going on and may even intercede. However, a PinLeader should never count on that level of awareness or care within the organization. The most effective leaders regularly refer to the agreed-upon plan. The plan becomes a tool that supports the leaders in applying the right amount of pressure to see the project through.

Accountability, reasonable deadlines, and scorecards that track how the organization is doing can help prevent a push with excessive force. It will also support even progress toward the goal. In other words, an effective strategic plan that accounts for these forces or stresses will help minimize the pressure. Surprises are good for holidays and birthdays, but are not ideal occurrences within an organization that wants to experience steady, sure progress toward its goals. Minimize surprises through periodic fact checking and the measurement of outcomes and goals in your organizational plan.

 PinPoint: Although not ideal, sometimes the only choice for an organization or a leader is to work with the bend. This situation may be the result of the lack of available resources or a limited set of options.

What if the bent pin is still in use? In such a case, a leader might recruit the help of another pin who can intercede in order to prevent project failure. The other leader can help course correct before permanent damage or misdirection occurs. This does not necessarily mean you throw the bent pin out, but consideration should be taken to see if pressure can be applied to get the bent pin back into shape.

To illustrate this point further, consider a time when you or others within your organization may have engaged in a discussion that concluded with an unexpected decision to bring another leader in to complete the work at hand or to lead a particular project. What was the rationale used to replace the existing leader? Have you ever heard statements made that imply someone or yourself was "too close to the situation" or "too passionate" about the project? Did the individual whose leadership was questioned remain with the organization?

Similar to the goal to embrace straightforwardness, there may need to be a pivot from one leader to another. Sometimes this pivot must occur based on a push that has been too forceful or which has resulted in too many pins being bent out of shape. Evaluation and review are an important part of project leadership.

Every great leader will eventually come across that one project she is passionately vested in. The key here again is self awareness paired with the ability to seek outside assistance where that could prove beneficial. The PinLeader will seek out assistance to get back into proper shape, enlisting the help of those she trusts to assist her in finding the right balance in terms of the push. After assistance is gained, the leader must be able to take the advice received and apply it.

Consider your options should you find yourself in a similar place. Could you approach a mentor or trusted friend and ask for their input? Add self-evaluation to the mix. How might you better ensure the degree of push on a current project or evaluate a recent project? Did you push the team too hard to get to the goal? What might you do to help get a derailed project back on track?

How can you tell if a pin has passed the point of no return to effective leadership? Can a pin ever get back to its original shape? There are definitive signs that a bent pin is getting back to its original shape. The ability to accept constructive criticism is one positive indicator. Allowing time and space for self reflection and the mastering skill of post-project evaluation are key. Finally, the evidence of clear action steps taken to get a project back on track is evidence of a pin on the mend.

The Broken Pin

We've now come to the worst scenario: the broken pin. In this case, the push has exhausted the leader to the point of no return. The leader's initial push may have placed that leader or the team into what they once viewed as the ideal situation. However, what may have been initially considered the ideal sometimes turns out to be not advantageous and to have serious unanticipated consequences. Sometimes, the leader finds there are factors that lie far outside of his control. In other situations, the factors become clear the goal that was set at the outset of the project was not appropriate.

The break can be slow or it can come quickly depending upon how hard the push is. If the push comes from external forces, the break may appear after it is determined the project is off track or the organization is deemed to be failing. Additional stress is experienced by those watching the break happen. A broken pin can also cause harm to the culture. Feelings of unsteadiness, insecurity, and anxiety may be prevalent. On the other side of such an experience, team members or employees may be relieved the break has happened.

An excessive push within any working situation may drive individuals to leave the organization. Unfortunately, the break may come too late, and those team members you wish would have stayed may have already been lured away from the organization or left on their own accord. This is why it is so imperative that leaders on the PinLeader Path take care to avoid a broken pin in terms of guarding their own leadership capacity and tending to the well-being of each contributor on their teams.

But isn't there a way to repair the broken pin? If you picture a pin broken either by the outside push or by the pressure of all it has to hold together, you know that a pin is done. It is important to understand that there are just times a person reaches the point of no return in an organization. Trust may be broken. Relationships may be unrepairable.

 PinPoint: Broken pins need time to be fixed and that means another opportunity or project. Jumping right into another project or a new organization could create repeated breaks and undesirable results. Leave the past in the past and seek assistance. Give consideration to those areas that negatively impacted the situation. Once this has been tended to, start fresh and maintain a positive approach.

Seeking assistance from other PinLeaders is a must for organizations where a leader has lost his or her motivation or drive. At times, a fresh perspective is just what a project or organization needs. Hope and the building of new connections can bring back the energy. However, leaders on the PinLeader Path must hit the ground running, bring their own level of push, and not hesitate to take corrective action to address past missteps. Without that confidence, there is most likely going to be a problem with keeping the project on track.

And what of the broken pin? Is there life after a perceived failure for that pin? Of course there is! Just because a push has resulted in the leader having to walk away does not mean that leader is not able to lead effectively or step into other opportunities. The difference comes in how the leader addresses the push. If the push was internal, then that leader can engage in self reflection and consider how the push impacted them as a leader. If the push was externally generated, the leader must decide if he or she wants to place himself or herself into a situation where the same level of push may be applied.

Being mindful around your perceptions of a push or shove applies here too. You may be aware of circumstances where a certain leader moves from organization to organization attempting to find the right fit. Leaders devoted to the PinLeader Path should consult those they trust, to include their own board of directors, for career development. Securing feedback from trusted sources before making the decision to leave a position or change organizations is advisable. Such a move may be necessary but, as the saying goes, the grass may not be greener on the other side.

 PinPoint: It is not the responsibility of the leader who is leaving to take team members with them. The leader should lend support for a transition, but team members should not expect a leader to take them along to their next assignment.

Another interesting point in the case of a broken pin comes as we consider those left behind. Those who remain on a project team or within the department or organization may be resentful that the break has occurred. They may have the desire to leave the project or organization. For those who decide to drive change on their own initiative or within the context of the project, the break may cause delays in their own work. Even where this is the case, opportunities are available to the PinLeader.

When that leader knows that he or she will not be able to bring the project to completion, fulfill expectations, or be successful, moving on is the best choice and one that should be embraced. It is too much to expect a leader to keep hanging on when the push or shove is inhibiting their effectiveness as a leader.

The three results of the excessive push—a pin becoming dull, bent, or broken—are each less than ideal. Excessive pushing has clear consequences and leads to undesirable results, but few are the organizations where such incidents do not occur. Knowing that too forceful a push is a possibility and understanding the consequences of such force can prepare PinLeaders and those across the organization to take steps to correct such situations when they occur.

But what of the placement of that pin? Can it be possible that pins are too close together? That the pins are "bumping" into one another? What if the pins are too far apart? Are there gaps to manage? Has the fabric been stretched too tight for stitching that will stand the test of time? All of these are important considerations.

Pin Placement Matters

There comes a time when a judgment call must be and will be made. Just as pins are positioned strategically on fabric in accordance with the pattern or desired sewing project, the placement of a leader is often based upon the best judgements made at that time. The pattern may call for a collection of pins but may not always provide instructions with regard to the precise number needed or exactly where to place the pins.

The same is true of effective leaders. An organization may know it needs multiple pins but where they are placed, what they are charged with holding or bringing together, and how long they have to hold that position makes a difference. Let's look at a few examples of the impact of those placements.

Too Crowded

In this scenario, there are just too many pins and they have been placed too tightly together. People are too close to work independently. Teams are over-saturated and there is an overlap in responsibilities. This closeness impedes the ability for the sewing needle to maneuver in order to get the permanent thread in place. On top of these difficulties, the crowded pins situation is very costly to the organization and a waste of top talent.

Perhaps you have witnessed a leader come into an organization and be placed next to another strong leader. However, instead of collaborating as administrators had hoped they would, the two leaders bump up against one another. They may even see each other as rivals. Each may covet the responsibility the other leader has been given. Often one leader will want resources allocated to the other leader, believing they would help them fulfill their role and responsibilities more efficiently.

What starts off of as a good idea to bring another leader in to work in tandem with the first leader within a department or on a project could spell disaster not only for that specific area but for the organization as a whole. Perhaps team members have witnessed or been involved with leaders who ask staff to select an area or take on a side project. Choice matters, but can such a choice truly be made of free will? A sense of loyalty and other expectations may come with that choice.

There are times when administrators may set up such a situation on purpose with the intention of creating competition to increase performance. Has that been successful? Yes, sometimes, but it does have significant consequences. Productivity may increase, but long-term results will flatten.

Every good leader has a competitive drive and sometimes that drive can be spurred on by a peer leader. Such a leader will eventually become bored if she continuously meet goals without much effort. Boredom can lead to restlessness. Restlessness can lead to looking around for the next opportunity. Ultimately competition also means someone is going to come in second. How is that second leader going to act? Is she going to remain happy? Most likely not and this may result in another bout of restlessness and thus the cycle happens with this leader too.

 PinPoint: Examine the reasons behind the desire to bring another leader into the organization to fulfill a similar role or to work in the same department. If there is a perceived problem, do not place more people or financial resources toward the problem until and unless you have thoroughly analyzed the situation and determined this is the only viable solution.

What if the costs to an organization are doubled? Having two leaders working in the same department or on the same project takes a delicate balance of understanding each leader's personality and motivations. If competitive, the salaries of the two PinLeaders will be comparable and in line with one another. If not, this too eventually creates a problem for the organization.

What if a sales culture and commission is involved? In some organizations, the strongest survive but has your organization considered mentoring and succession planning with a sales commission culture? Perhaps the whole organization is cut out for handling this approach to culture. However, if you are interjecting or imposing a sales and commission scenario and it was not expected, this could also drive out not only the leaders out also the staff and teams that report to that leader. Most organizations are not flush with cash and do not have the ability to make such costly mistakes.

The essential question to ask when considering hiring another leader to do a similar job as another leader is why? Is there a lack of confidence or trust in the current leader? Was there a request to get someone in to replace the current leader? If there is a challenge within the department in question, bringing in another leader sends a message to the entire staff as well.

This approach of throwing additional resources toward a challenge is not always the best solution. It is recommended that hiring managers analyze the rationale for a suggestion that another leader be brought on board first. This will allow them to uncover the source of any problem. Based on the information gleaned from such an inquiry, if it is determined that another pin is needed, it is often best to fully replace the original PinLeader than to crowd or confuse that leader.

Too Far Apart

What about the opposite effect? Can pins be too far apart? What if there are pins holding the fabric together that seem disjointed from the rest? If the gaps are wide, will the material hold together long enough to allow the thread to come through?

The gaps that divide us can be our undoing. Imagine you have been assigned a team and given goals, but you are unsure about how these goals contribute to the overall strategic plan. What if you know other leaders are working on pieces of an overall plan but you do not know their goals or understand how your work interplays or interfaces with theirs? There are so many stories of these types of gaps. Let's consider how such gaps occur within organizations. We will focus on the two main reasons gaps occur, which relate to budget and poor communication.

Budget Considerations, Costs, and Cuts

Any time there appears to be too few leaders, it typically is the result of budget cuts. Most organizations understand the need to have leaders strategically placed to produce the best outcomes but this takes resources. A full analysis is necessary in order to understand what is the right distance between leaders and know how resources should be allocated. The right budget and the right balance of leaders will vary depending on the specific needs and goals of each organization.

But what if the analysis reveals that cost cutting has reduced efficiency or has created a negative culture full of doubt, worry, and a lack of innovation? The consequence of continuous cost cutting is leaders who bend beneath the constant pressure to perform with little or no resources provided. Those leaders are forced to look for other ways to reach goals, and sometimes the easiest path is not the best path.

Another consequence of the cycle of cost-cutting measures comes when leaders make promises today that they "hope" they do not have to deal with in the future. These leaders may sign contracts that include "balloon payments," with lower investments required in the first two years and major jumps in payment amounts a few years later. They may begin to rely on organizations, books, groups, or individuals who sell them one-size-fits-all solutions to their questions. None of these are ideal approaches to determining how many leaders are needed to reach organizational goals. The most effective method is a *customized* approach.

A more prudent ways to determine the right balance of leaders required comes when an organization's leadership chooses to do the following:

- lean into peers and their organizations,

- ask already positioned PinLeaders who are impacted, and

- bring another leader on board, perhaps using a consultant from outside the organization who does not benefit from the structure.

This is also the time to ask questions about what the actual financial investment in leadership looks like. Investment is the key word here. A direct return on investment may not happen quickly and may not be as evident in the months and years after making a new hire. Keeping close ties to the human resource department in order to understand retention, talking to front-line employees about morale, and consulting with the finance department on efficiency and sales goals are some of the measures that can be taken when it comes to considering the costs associated with placing PinLeaders.

Communication

Who decided a change was needed? How are we supposed to get this all done? Why are we doing it this way? Who is really calling the shots? No one asked me and I do this job every day. If you have heard sayings like these from teams in your organization, are a part of a group where these sentiments have been expressed, or know employees in your organization are saying something similar (perhaps even about you), there is a problem.

Many employees participate in water cooler discussions attempting to find out what is going on and, most importantly, to determine what is coming next. Having even one of every four employees not knowing what the plan is and what part they play in that plan can derail forward movement for the organization. Frequent discussions and gossip about any change in direction or leadership within the organization is the hallmark of poor communications within that organization.

The first thought is that if poor communication exists, it could have arisen because there are not enough leaders to share the information or to stop misinformation from feeding into the organization's channels. This could be a correct assessment. The space between pins creates a gap. A lack of connectedness between leaders who do have an understanding of the big picture can do the same.

However, there is another reason for the existence of gossip in the workplace and that is poor communicators. If organizational leaders do not take the time to work on their own interpersonal communications, the result will be gaps of information. Such gaps inevitably lead to either rumors to fill those gaps (sometimes true and sometimes not) or to negative impacts on staff who are just working to work and who do not have a clearly defined or articulated purpose.

Leaders have a responsibility to make their engagement with teams a worthwhile and meaningful experience for everyone. Transparency and clarity must be a part of the overall communication strategy. That strategic approach is part of being straightforward and a demonstration of strength of character. This approach includes engaging in two-way conversations that place listening at the very heart of any discussion.

PINLEADER INTERACTIVE

Join the PinLeader Path Community! Scan the QR code below to access the PinLeader Interactive. Use the following questions for further discussion and consideration.

The Case of the Push

- Has there been a time when you were not sure where the "push" was coming from? Were you motivated even more or less in that situation?

- What do you value the most in team members— experience or education? Does it change depending on the situation? Why?

- Have you ever picked up a project from a previous leader? How did you feel about it? Was it a positive or negative experience? What was the outcome?

- What advice would you give leaders if they feel they have pushed too far? Have you ever been in such a situation?

- What motivates you?

CHAPTER 7: **Culture and Organizational Fabric**

It all began with the new strategic plan. The plan that everyone was waiting for. The plan that was supposed to set new goals for the organization and prepare it for growth. The plan that each prior leader had talked about for years. The plan that was built from the inside and was supposed to bring departments together. The plan that would save jobs and might even create new ones. The plan that was to guide the organization for the next five years.

Charles was glad to lead the strategic planning process. He had been tapped by his leadership to implement it immediately. Although he was given a sizable budget, he had barely spent any of it. After all, everyone had been waiting for this for almost four years now. Charles knew it was his time to shine. He was ready to demonstrate he could lead not only his own department but that of the entire organization under the direction of the president. He felt confident that he had the backing of senior leadership.

He began having meetings to discuss the plan with the different departments. He had both his agenda and copies of the plan accessible digitally in a drop folder and also provided hard copy. This seemed simple enough. However, shortly after passing out the plan at an early meeting, many of the attending departments questioned where the goals for their departments had originated.

The department members reviewed the measurements and stated that these benchmarks were too high. They believed the plan did not accurately represent the work they did and how they did it and suggested modifications. Department members shared they were worried that they would be held accountable to the lofty goals contained in the plan. Furthermore, those members who were chosen to be in meetings with Charles began to ask for and review other departments goals and measurements and stated that the goals seemed "too low" and did not seem as demanding as those set for their own department.

Charles listened to the concerns and then set up a meeting with his senior leadership team to explain the situation. The senior leadership team listened to him but reminded him that the plan had been created from within and had been approved. Now was the time to implement.

Charles decided to complete the rest of his meetings and found similar stories coming from the impacted departments. Simply no one wanted to commit to the goals and assigned action items. The theme of the concerns expressed remained consistent—the plan did not reflect what the departments actually did, these departments did not have the resources to accomplish the goal assigned to them, and the relevancy of the plan remained in question by many who attended these meetings.

Charles did some research to discover the origins of the current plan. He found a record of a "task force" for the plan and noted that more than half of the names of those on the list were no longer with the organization. The remainder were in place but were in leadership positions overseeing departments across the organization, but the former task force members were not involved in client-facing interactions on a daily basis. Charles' conclusion? The plan did not take into account the culture of each department, nor did it accurately reflect what those respective departments did.

Charles had skills with strategic planning but did not have proven experience motivating teams or pivoting a plan. The lack of these skills put him in an untenable situation. Nevertheless, the organization's leadership was adamant: the plan had been approved and the plan should be implemented. The voices of those in departments across the organization were equally as insistent. Across the organization, department leaders believed the plan was flawed and the majority of the department members and teams Charles had discussed the plan with were not on board with moving forward.

PinLeader Considerations

- What do you think Charles should do?

- Should he seek outside help? Why or why not?

- What are the challenges or potential downside would Charles might face if he chooses to enforce the plan despite the stated concerns?

Culture Types

Charles is facing a dilemma that he cannot solve alone. He wants to be straightforward, but he needs to understand how to pivot. He needs to know how to navigate this critical juncture in the planning process. One viable option is to seek the external assistance needed to successfully modify the plan. To do that, however, Charles must present solid reasons why consulting with experts or partnering with an outside organization may be necessary.

His first goal should be to build rapport with the departments and to understand what they do and how they do it. A hands-on partner organization might help him build trust so that the departments will respond to and engage with him and his team. Charles has a desire to follow the PinLeader Path, but he also needs help setting timetables.

Just as any sewing project that needs one or several pins to hold the cloth in place, within organizations the first step is to determine what type of fabric and the cut of the cloth you are working with. You must consider the composition or makeup of the cloth and its unique properties. What pressures can the fabric take? What amount of pressure may well unravel the threads woven together to create the fabric?

Situations such as the one faced by Charles, a new leader seeking to implement a strategic plan he did not develop, can happen in every workplace and department. Charles must address the clear concerns. He must acknowledge and address the disconnect between the perspective of various departments charged with implementing goals they do not believe to be reasonable and the perspective of the organization's top leadership.

Such pressure points are often revealed when groups from across the organization come together. Teams have the opportunity to build rapport when they spend time together and choose to learn from one another. When groups from across the organization convene, existing pressures often become evident, just as we saw in the example of Charles and the long-awaited strategic plan. Patterns are both revealed and created from the synergies that naturally occur in such cross-functional environments. This is culture. Culture is as old as time, and it will change over time.

We often hear the word culture when we discuss groups of individuals with similar lived experiences. Culture is represented in a number of ways like when we speak about groups who get together to play cards or when we discuss our favorite sports teams and their athletic programs. Each of us is part of many cultures. We may even create places for a new culture to flourish when we come together with others or engage with various groups. We often gravitate toward people who think like us because we believe we have something in common with them. We might say these people and groups are "cut from the same piece of cloth" as are we.

These biases and beliefs inform the culture as do the qualities of the threads that make up the fabric. Those threads represent each individual that makes up the team. By itself, a thread can easily be broken but together, and with a higher number of strands that are interwoven or integrated together, the fabric becomes stronger. The fabric metaphor lends itself nicely as a way to describe organizational cultures that have distinct features and ways of operating and unique approaches. But are there other reasons why the concept of fabric is commonly used as a synonym to describe culture?

Fabric is one of the best known items in our everyday lives. People need and use cloth and fabric on a daily basis. We are familiar with the various textures and feeling of a variety of materials used to construct our clothing. Fabric is incorporated into many of the products we use. It is built into the chairs and sofas where we sit. Some fabric is thin and easily worked with, while other fabrics are difficult to manage and not easily penetrated, no matter how sharp or strong the pin. Even where there is a straight plan to follow, in some cases the fabric may prove too tough to manage—even for one who is skilled at working with a variety of pins and fabric types.

Fabric comes in different styles, colors, and types with varying attributes, such as those found in silk, cotton, wool, leather, and synthetic. Let's consider a few common culture types at play in today's organizational landscape.

Soft as Silk Culture Type

Let's examine a department that employees transitioned in and out of very easily. In this department, operations seem smooth and the team players seem to operate as one seamless unit. There are two main reasons for this: either the organization has a great culture or it has a poor culture with no gray areas. In the latter scenario, individuals are either in or they are out based on their own decisions or that of the organization.

For those silk-like cultures that are indeed great places to work, participants often experience an easy onboarding process. Everyone in the department helps the new person with their questions and provides direction and input on shared processes and common practices. This culture reflects a graceful mentality with forgiveness at its core. Where mistakes are made, they are gently corrected.

Just as sharp pins easily penetrate a smooth silk cloth, leaders can easily influence and direct a department that has a Soft as Silk Culture (SSC). When pinning the unique fabric of this departmental culture with other units that have a similar culture, the work is easy as long as the leader has a steady hand and applies careful handling to avoid a tear in the delicate fabric. The leaders walking the PinLeader Path in a Soft as Silk Culture work to keep processes running smoothly with open communication. They motivate individuals by indicating how their work impacts strategic plans and is needed in the organization.

In this culture, gossip and backbiting behaviors are kept at a minimum. Positive attitudes coupled with teamwork are at the core of this culture type. However, without constant diligence and clear communication that addresses any issues that may arise between team members, this culture can become fragile quite quickly.

The silk-like culture that is less than ideal has many of the attributes of the ideal Soft as Silk Culture, to include quick onboarding into the department or organization. However, in the less than ideal silk-like culture, the leader does not have the three core PinLeader qualities and may be "forcing" workloads, micromanaging, and withholding information from the team. When a pin is pushed roughly through silk, a hole can form. This creates an undesirable result and a tear in the fabric. A similar outcome can be expected when a leader is operating with force.

Cultures that exhibit holes will often have many team members quickly exiting the department. Areas within the organization with this type of culture are typically avoided by those within the organization who are considering a change, and many individuals within these departments may begin to exhibit a laissez-faire attitude. The under-functioning department with a Soft as Silk Culture does not work well with other departments or organizations. Outsiders may observe that the department "appears" to be a desirable one, but those vested in joining will soon discover it may be the opposite.

> **PinPoint:** The saying that the "grass is greener on the other side" is partly true in the sense that it may indeed appear greener. In some cases the illusion of a better culture is created by putting up a false front. The "grass" may simply be spray painted. Leaders must do their research and be prepared for any circumstance before going into a situation. If it appears "too good to be true" investigate further. It is perfectly fine to be cautious. This is the way of the wise PinLeader.

Leaders on the PinLeader Path should be prepared to find ways to motivate and encourage their team members. Since an impoverished or undernourished Soft as Silk Culture (SSC) may have been the result of prior ineffective leadership, a PinLeader should work to build back trust. The focus should be on co-creating positive relationships and acknowledging contributions from the group and its members. Setting deadlines and demonstrating ties to the strategic plan are also of critical importance and help reinforce purpose throughout the department.

Breathable as Cotton Culture Type

Ever experienced going into an organization or department and just knowing you would "fit in" with the culture there? You may have quickly observed that the people working there share similar likes and interests. You can sense that you will be respected and able to contribute in such an easy-going environment. Perhaps you can even enjoy the work and relax a little as you move into your workspace each day. The Breathable as Cotton Culture (BCC) has the properties of being breathable, light, and easy to wear. This type of environment is similar to the fabric we know as cotton—a fabric known for being durable and renewable with a 100 percent ability to be recycled.

Cotton is described as having a high absorption rate. This fabric can be printed on and even dyed without losing its breathable properties. Now, think of departments or organizations with similar properties in their culture. How do pins that are strong, straight, and sharp work with cotton? The Breathable as Cotton Culture is one team members can move into easily and in which they can remain connected to those around them.

This culture type remains strong and durable in spite of frequent changes. New branding and marketing may well impact the image of the department or organization, but the core culture remains intact. Most importantly, a Breathable as Cotton Culture can be easily replicated because it is substantial enough and holds credibility. It has been tested over time and has proven its worth and reliability. Other departments or organizations want this culture, because employees want to be wrapped in a place where they can breathe and have room to grow.

 PinPoint: Although some cultures can withstand and absorb significant levels of change well, a leader should not take this for granted. Change that occurs at a high level of impact, such as mergers or changes in products or service within a tight timeframe or with the added demands of a quick turnaround can be quite stressful. Monitoring for stress is prudent and multiple supports should be put in place in every culture, regardless of its type or characteristics.

What has been described so far about this culture type takes into account the fact that cotton is wearable. However, cotton has one other property that makes it highly valued and that is its absorbency. The Breathable as Cotton Culture can take in the bad with the good and still progress toward a goal. This is a highly valuable asset for any department or organization. Employees in these cultures do not dwell in negativity. Rather, they listen and reflect, considering whether the information being communicated is relevant to their role within the organization.

Additionally, the Breathable as Cotton Culture displays the characteristic of being flexible. Any PinLeader working with this culture will find that team members not only absorb different types of information and news but that change is expected within this culture type. Leaders operating in this culture understand that change can happen any day. They are not wedded to one specific method. Innovation and creativity thrive in these departments and organizations.

Because the team members are likely to be close to one another, they are encouraged and support one another. If there is a comment that targets one team member in a negative way, it is likely that the team will come together to support that member. Leaders should prepare to not only keep the Breathable as Cotton Culture informed with routine communication but also engage this group with challenging projects that tap their diverse skills and experiences for solution-based outcomes.

The Functional as Wool Culture Type

What about a culture where everyone knew one another but had been attracted to the department or organization for other reasons? Have you ever heard anyone explain that they chose a department or an organization because they feel secure there? Or perhaps you were able to get into such a position but, once you were in place, it seemed much harder to work there than you had expected.

Some types of cultures seem attractive because there seems to be a level of warmth and comfort involved. In the Functional as Wool Culture (FWC), this is just a perception or first impression. Playing into the need for team members to be safe and secure, this culture type has the same properties, both positive and negative, as the fabric of wool.

The need to have a sense of security is not new. Some organizations attract employees based on this with need. These organizations may make promises of pensions, contracts, and rewards or guarantee a consistent paycheck. Individuals may take on new roles simply based on that level of protection or safety. Functional as Wool Cultures tend to thrive when they are financially solvent, but once there are issues with profits they will begin to make changes in personnel benefits.

If the main reason an individual joined the organization is to obtain financial security, those individuals with the education and means to do so may leave the organizations at such junctures and move on to another opportunity. Leaders following the PinLeader Path who lead departments or organizations where a Functional as Wool Culture is in place may find that there is a commitment to the organization but not necessarily to the mission. A sharp pin is needed but most importantly one that is straight with the ability to pivot.

 PinPoint: The property of absorption is found in several types of cloths and cultures. Keep in mind that whatever is being absorbed will impact the project. Leaders must be mindful of this fact and ensure that transparent and truthful information is disseminated on a regular basis.

Another characteristic of the Functional as Wool Culture is the appearance that it is "insulated" and resistant to change. Just as woven wool provides warmth and protection against the elements and we perceive wool to be insulating, so too this culture type appears to be impervious to undue outside influence. In such cultures, change is unlikely to occur easily. This culture type will absorb and even share all types of information but because there is a perception that no change will ultimately happen. When change does occur, it can be devastating to those in the department or organization. Individuals who sought out the comfort of the organization may be surprised and may overreact or, alternatively, not react at all but choose to remain in denial that change is imminent or even occurring.

Examples of an overreaction include but are not limited to quitting, speaking poorly about the change occurring within the department or organization, and discouraging other individuals from joining the team, department, or group. In extreme cases, some longtime members of a Functional as Wool Culture may even threaten those around them with a behavior that would not be what would be expected by that individual. Leaders who come into this culture should build in professional development for managing organizational change for team members, encourage ongoing communication, and prepare for potential negative reactions.

In the case of the Functional as Wool Culture, where there often is no reaction or there is an outright denial that a change is occurring, leaders may observe a range of detrimental behaviors. Individuals within such cultures may "silently quit" and cease to offer ideas or contribute input or solutions to problems, even when these are solicited and encouraged. An employee in the Functional as Wool Culture may openly state that he or she will not be doing more than what the job description says. Team members may mutiny, assuming an attitude of complete control and making predictions about what they know will happen next. They may consider even themselves to be above and beyond the reach of negative consequences for their actions.

Those following a PinLeader Path should include professional development as a tool with such cultures but not expect that this alone will manage undesirable behaviors. Consistent communication that conveys facts and supports for needed changes will be the most effective approach.

Unfortunately, in either extreme in terms of reaction and response to change, there will be a high percentage of those who may want to leave in a Functional as Wool Culture.

The Tough as Leather Culture Type

Picture a department that has remained relatively unchanged in terms of its people and operations for many years. Potentially the same individuals are in place for many years in such cultures. What might happen when someone new enters that department or area where there is a natural toughness?

Have you seen such a situation in a culture that seemed unchanged? Did it take a long time for the group to accept the new team member? Did anyone ever use the word "fit" when describing new employees or team members they hoped would join? Did a new recruit leave the department before anyone expected them to do so?

This is the Tough as Leather Culture. In such cultures, there are departments that are nearly impenetrable. The department leadership may even boast about this aspect of their culture and comment on how hard it is to get in. The leadership may take pride in "screening" individuals and only consider a certain type of individual as worthy of the opportunity. If the opportunity for inclusion within a group is highly competitive and must be earned through one's own merit, activity, education, or experience that is a different circumstance.

In such cases, the culture is deservingly pegged as a "good but tough" culture. However, if culture is derived by acceptance based on perceived popularity, what others can gain from allowing them in, or some type of legacy not based on merit, the culture may be tough, but it is one that is impoverished and in some ways unhealthy.

Any leader attempting to lead a Tough as Leather Culture or build a team with new members coming into the organization that has this culture type must have the best of all three attributes of strength, sharpness, and a straight to the point plan that can penetrate that strong leather-like culture. A continuous push by the leader will eventually get it done, but leaders must recognize that bringing this culture type together with other groups will require strong pins who can work together with this type of culture group.

 PinPoint: Like tough leather, cultures that are strong have a sense of purpose and understand their contributions. Leaders should continue to reinforce this intentionality and functionality, motivating members to keep up the good work.

If a leader can work with the positive attributes of the culture, this culture can weather a change well. Just as leather fabric is not easily torn when pins come and go, a Tough as Leather Culture will generally maintain its shape when pushed and pulled. Keeping team members in this culture informed and involving the members in the process of change will result in positive outcomes and more effective teams.

Synthetic Culture Type

Each of the organic fabrics we have mentioned have their pros and cons. One fabric might be too heavy but does a great job of being durable. Another fabric may be light but needs extra care and is easily torn. One fabric may need a sharper, stronger pin and other may rely on the sharpness and straightness to hold the pieces together.

But what happens when the elements are combined to create a new fabric or culture within the organization? The qualities of one fabric type blended with another leaves the original challenges of each culture type in place. However, by tapping into the ability to artificially create a fabric, it is possible to weave together the most desirable characteristics from several culture types and eliminate unwanted attributes.

Just as synthetic fabrics have introduced new options in terms of clothing, the Synthetic Culture Type can offer benefits to a department or organization. As with fabric, cultures that are artificially developed often have positive attributes. Imagine a team that can generate solutions within seconds, never argue among themselves, perform task after task without rest, and take direction without complaint?

Artificial intelligence (AI) lends itself to teams as a companion and support. AI can be a great "team player" in an organization. AI may not be perfect, but it does attempt to take the human bias out of decision-making, and these attributes can provide positive results. AI pulls from its growing database of knowledge. It has the innate ability to obtain new information almost instantly without getting dull or experiencing any shrinkage from processing in a micro way.

Like cotton, artificial intelligence is highly durable. Because it is always learning and updating its knowledge base, it is likely to resist becoming stagnant or is unlikely to be affected by environmental dangers like mildew. Like nylon, polyester, and spandex, AI has the ability to be flexible and stretchable. Due to its lack of emotions, AI does not fear change. It simply computes solutions around that change. Situations may arise that may leave a human team stunned and create a pause where AI reacts quickly, allowing any downpour of information to roll right off.

However, the very attribute that makes AI useful as a new team player is also its inherent challenge. In the world of human interaction building trust and relationships is a valuable asset. PinLeaders are exceptionally good at building connections and will outperform AI in this capacity. AI serves as a reliable source of information, but enlisting AI to work *with* other teams may prove to be a challenge.

The language used between machines in the Synthetic Culture type is different than communication between a machine and humans. Those characteristics that make us human including emotions, humor, and creativity expressed through lived experiences are still critical components of culture. In other words, organic fabric is still viewed as a high quality.

These characteristics lend personality and strength to a team. When reaching an audience or client base, having that connection and empathy with them is also part of the equation.

Leaders should be clear on what they hope to accomplish by being in a Synthetic Culture group utilizing AI and ensure that they reflect on the benefits of artificial intelligence, focusing on cases where AI excels over the performance of human team members. As AI learns and becomes more proficient, interactions with Synthetic Culture group types will become more similar to interactions between humans. In the not too distant future, the Synthetic Culture group type may become more prevalent and it will not be surprising to see a team composed of both human and AI team members.

While the complexities of this are challenging, such collaboration can potentially creatively shift organizational culture. Although this discussion extends beyond the scope of our focus in this book, working with the Synthetic Culture group type is a challenge that leaders must consider as they themselves navigate this monumental change for business and for our culture at large.

The Elements

We've examined the impact of the pin and the types of cloth but have not yet considered the external elements that impact the cloth. In some cases, the elements at play in the immediate environment may directly impact the characteristics of the fabric or culture, making it either more difficult or easier to work with. In the same way, the leader must bring their full awareness to how they handle the fabric and keep it from being negatively impacted by the environment. The most seasoned leaders make the creation of a positive work environment, its nourishment and its safeguarding a priority. The leader's ability to be sharp, strong, and straight on point may be impacted by these elements.

The elements of water and heat are the two main environmental factors that affect fabric or cloth. Consider a time when you may have placed an item of clothing in the dryer only to discover later that you had shrunk it. Or perhaps you got an item wet and then discovered after the fact that it appeared to feel and look different from when you bought it. Organizations go through their own type of expansion and shrinkage. Those that successfully "weather the elements" thrive. Let's take a look a few examples of what the most common environmental impacts might mean for leaders and their teams.

The Heat Resistant Fabric

Depending on the material, heat can change the composition of the fabric. Heat can melt or burn the cloth. Heat can also change the form of a liquid to gas, potentially a poisonous one, that seeps into the fabric. Heat can create beauty. Such is the case with wool. When heat is applied to wool, it turns into felt.

A circumstance that impacts an organization in such a way that requires the team to pull together to meet a challenge head on can lead to a similar outcome. The leader on the PinLeader Path may have to pull heavily on all his attributes of sharp, strength, and straightforward planning to manage the heat. With that PinLeader goal met, the organization emerges stronger and often in a more attractive state that it was before the challenge occurred.

What if the fabric was heat resistant? What if the fabric could take the heat and still keep its shape and form? What if it was so tough that it protected whoever was wearing it from any effect from the heat? Some cultures are heat resistant. Whatever is tossed at the culture, whether the heat of major budget cuts, the loss of a beloved leader, or an unforeseen acquisition, the group performs well and keeps moving toward their goals. PinLeaders who lead organizations cut from this type of cloth will find resilience and the passion to keep moving among its members.

With certain fabric and culture types, expecting departments or organizations to continue to perform with repeated changes and quick turnarounds will eventually wear the resistance out. The PinLeader learns to continuously monitor and assess the durability and state of strength within their teams. As leaders provide care to these groups, they must also be ready to take on the heat themselves. They must stand prepared to help shield those within the organization whenever possible.

After the heat, or whatever has placed the organization in a challenging position, is gone it is time reflect and learn from the circumstance. This is where some organizations miss the opportunity to uncover the root causes of challenges so that the organization can better prepare for the future. PinLeaders view the heat as an opportunity for learning and preparation, guiding their teams to become more heat resistant in the process.

The Water Repellant Fabric

If the fabric gets wet, water changes the dynamics of how that fabric functions and can be handled. If no repellant is present, the cloth can get soaked. The process of drying out the fabric must occur if the material is to be used successfully again. Without appropriate time to allow the fabric to dry thoroughly, there will be a risk of shrinkage and mildew. Now, imagine if this piece of clothing was an organizational culture. Imagine there was no protection against the constant "dumping" of jobs and responsibilities. The culture gets soaked with more and more to do even though its members cannot perform their basic duties.

Leaders responsible for tending to these cultures may find burnout and a lack of hope that things will ever change as common experiences among team members. Leaders may start out sharp and strong by sitting in a culture that is stagnate can eventually rust and compromise the pin. If mold occurs within this culture, leaders may not be able to salvage it.

In such situations, those in these cultures will soon find a way to exit. But what if this material were water repellant? Those organizations that have these characteristics are all the more prepared and will weather all types of downpours. And like a pin that is strong, water repellant cloth will not allow a pin to rust. This allows the integrating of the pin. Think of a time when you thought a leader was in a situation you believed he simply could not recover from but somehow he came back even stronger. This did not occur by chance. Most likely that leader prepared for a "rainy day" and ensured he was diversified and well prepared to find new avenues.

In some circumstances the materials of a fabric or culture are not water repellant at all, but can somehow absorb whatever comes along. In fact, some fabric has the ability to not absorb more than it can take on without losing its shape. In a culture, team members might deflect demands made on them. "No, we can't" is used not in a defiant way but rather as practical protection against what the culture knows it cannot successfully withstand or accomplish with the resources the culture currently has. The likelihood is that this culture is led by a leader following the PinLeader Path—a leader who knows and understands the breaking points of his team. Such a leader is well positioned to negotiate terms and to maintain a level of realistic expectation about what can be accomplished.

What happens after absorption has met its limits? Like any cloth that is now past its ability to absorb, there is a need to wring out the fabric and allow it to dry. In any organization, the culture needs assistance to adjust once the rain stops or a change has passed. People need to recoup and refocus. The culture itself needs to get back to its original shape or purpose. This takes time. It also requires the grace and empathy that only someone with a PinLeader mindset can provide.

Is there risk of shrinkage or loss of workforce? Is there a chance of mildew? Is there a fear of pausing too long or taking some action that might make the organization stagnant? Yes. But rain is inevitable, and not every day can be sunny. When a culture has absorbed a great deal of change, rest and respite are required.

How Access to Resources Informs Culture

Imagine a piece of cloth that is frayed and barely threaded together. The cloth naturally has a problem with holding its shape. Or think about a piece of fabric that has such a high thread count that it is extremely soft to touch. What about the cloth that has an "average" thread count, making it much more affordable yet still viable to do the job it was intended to do? What about the type of leader? Does the degree of the leader being sharp, strong, and straightforward make a difference on how he handles different levels of resources?

Just as fabric can be woven with various thicknesses and types of thread, so too an organization's culture is impacted by its access to resources. Consider for example a situation within an organization or department where individual thread types represent the financial, personnel, and artificial intelligence resources available. Such resources make a difference and directly impact the effectiveness of the team.

Leaders who have chosen to follow the PinLeader Path will carefully consider resources and advocate for additional support for their teams.

For each level and type of resource, there are unique approaches that can be employed in order to effectively manage teams and the projects assigned to them. Let's consider the three most common scenarios within organizations—the low thread count culture, the average thread count culture, and the high thread count culture.

The Low Thread Count Culture

Like a piece of cloth that is so thin you can almost see through it, teams working in a culture that has little to no resources cannot perform at their highest potential. Such cultures, called the Low Thread Count Culture, are the most likely to have trouble not only functioning on their own but also working with other teams. Limited resources and the inability to gain support to shore up efforts and meet goals in a timely manner creates frustration among members of this culture type. In such a case, the characteristic of straightforwardness is even more important. The leaders will need to be strategic about what commitments they can make for the team even as they continue to advocate for outside resources to be allocated.

Another characteristic of the Low Thread Count Culture is the lack of durability. Since team members are working with little to no resources, their attitudes concerning workloads will most likely not be as favorable. Leaders should take care in such a culture to reinforce the value of the work put into meeting goals by the team and its members, who have limited access to resources. Appreciation of the team's resourcefulness and persistence is critical. Additionally, leaders should pursue professional development for those within a culture where access to resources is limited. Leaders on the PinLeader Path who stay sharp will have connections external to the organization and should stay current on opportunities for staff.

The Average Thread Count Culture

Not everyone or department is cut from the same cloth. One size does not fit all when it comes to organizational cultures. Even pursuing the most minimal resources that meet the basic needs of completing a project or goal takes effort and awareness. This type of culture would be an Average Thread Count Culture. Having an average amount of thread count brings more substance to the cloth than that of the Low Thread Count Culture. The group experiences an improved ability to work with the culture in such cases.

The downside of having just enough resources to get the work done is there is that this may impede creativity or experimentation. Where innovation is limited, the results may fall short of desired outcomes. PinLeaders in an Average Thread Count Culture environment should set expectations based on the resources they have but understand that they will need to advocate for additional resources. This ability to access those additional resources allows leaders on the PinLeader Path to open up new pathways to identify innovative solutions and achieve stated goals.

As with the Low Thread Count Culture, in the Average Thread Count Culture professional development remains an important asset. Leaders should stay away from out of the box solutions and trainings for this culture type, which requires greater stimulation. Forms, policies, and handbooks have their place, but the vision and mission need to be incorporated and woven throughout any and all training initiatives. Leaders working with this culture type needs to drive toward excellence. That reach toward excellence helps take the "average" out of culture and increases the likelihood that the team will reach the next level of customization and growth that employees and contributors deserve.

 PinPoint: Do not use out of the box training programs, especially those that are online, with the Average Thread Count Culture. While there are successful formulas that can positively impact this culture type, programs must be customized by those who are trained on how to modify a curriculum successfully.

The High Thread Count Culture

The most valuable and highly prized fabric or culture has a high thread count. This is the most durable, softest, and strongest cloth known as the High Thread Count Culture. Members of groups within this culture type have greater access to resources and are typically perceived to be deserving of them.

Leaders that are on the PinLeader Path are most likely to obtain or manage these types of cultures over a period of time through demonstration of consistent and competent leadership. Within an organization, other teams may want to work with the High Thread Count Culture department or group in hopes of sharing these valuable resources. However, the reasons why this group is deserving may also be based on popularity and not necessarily on a clear demonstration of value.

Consider a situation where a department or organization secures a higher budget allocation based on perceptions of what organizational leaders think that team can do. Did the team accomplish what they set out to do? Perhaps. But in some cases they may have forecasted wrong, gone well over budget, or failed to hit their targets because team members did not have the skills to accomplish the goal. Leaders who have access to ample and abundant resources in terms of people, budget, or technologies such as artificial intelligence still need to strategize about how they can best utilize these resources.

In a number of circumstances, departments are measured by their spending. Too much spending means that the leadership does not plan well. Conversely, excess left in budgets at the end of a budget cycle may send a message that the leaders did not allocate resources appropriately. Either way, it falls on the leader to do his or her best in forecasting what resources are needed or required. If forecasting is not done well, what happens during the next budget cycle? Leaders will be more likely to allocate a smaller budget with fewer resources to the project or goal.

How does the unequal allocation of resources impact other areas of the organization? How do departments witnessing a higher allocation of resources to the High Thread Count Culture react? Strife and bitterness may follow if budgets appear lopsided. Leaders cannot lose sight of the big picture. Leaders who are strong and straightforward about their plan should communicate why budgets are allocated as they are. The PinLeader knows what is needed to get the best result and is able to make the case for proper budget allocation.

An understanding of the culture type will assist a leader to take the first step in working with those who are embedded in the organization. This understanding equips leaders to form strong relationships and build trust with their teams while also keeping their commitment to carry out plans and complete the scope of work for which they and their teams are responsible. Knowing how a culture might react to change is another important part of success. With this knowledge, the leader can guide and support the reactions of the team. Finally, success is also driven by how well a culture is supported by both human capital and financial resources.

PINLEADER INTERACTIVE

Join the PinLeader Path Community! Scan the QR code below to access the PinLeader Interactive. Use the following questions for further discussion and consideration.

The Case of the Culture Type

- Which of the types of cultures outlined here do you prefer? Why is this your preference?

- What would you suggest to a leader if he or she were challenged with a culture that they felt uncomfortable or even unwelcome in?

- What are the characteristics of the best training programs you have participated in? What did you learn in them?

- What are the characteristics of the worst training programs? How would you improve them?

CHAPTER 8: **Thread it All Together**

Mark knew he had something special. He created his company to fill a gap in the supply chain for a client. Now, as that client grew so did his own company. Mark took pride in telling some of his entrepreneur friends about the growth. He especially loved to share that he had maintained a low turnover and that most of the employees he had brought on expressed that they "loved" working for the company.

His client was glad to see Mark grow as well. Mark had expanded his service offerings, and the client noted that he had top notch customer service interactions with the assigned account representative. Mark had started his company with just one part-time employee but, to keep up with the demand created by a new client, within just two years the company had grown to forty full-time employees.

Mark managed his business by what he referred to as a "hands-on, family business" approach. He would join his human resources director for each job candidate interview and insisted on being the one to extend the offer to the successful interviewee with a handshake. He got to know each employee and kept up with their birthdays, marriages, and even the births or adoption of children. HR was directed to make sure birthday cards were sent out for every employee. Mark also requested that an internal newsletter be created to highlight employee family happenings including marriages, births, graduations, and acknowledging the duration of each employee's service to the company. He considered each one of his employees as family.

The productivity of the company was at such a high level that Mark felt comfortable having his Vice President of Operations take over. With day to day operations running smoothly, Mark began to take more vacations. He had full trust in his employees and, through an annual engagement survey conducted by an outside consulting group, he had full confidence that his employees trusted him in equal measure.

Mark's reputation grew in the community. He was seen as a solid business owner, recognized by the local Chamber of Commerce as someone who had created a great work environment. Mark was asked to speak, mentor up and coming entrepreneurs, and provide insights on how to create a positive work culture. He created Friday Fun Time, effectively shutting the business down at 4 p.m. at the end of each work week, when he provided hot dogs, chips, drinks, and someone to manage a grill for the weekly cookout.

During his third year, Mark picked up two additional clients and realized he would need to nearly double his staff. After speaking with HR and knowing his time was now more limited, he decided to forgo being so fully engaged in the hiring process. Instead, he opted to leave the hiring to the HR director to manage. He also noticed budgets had doubled and saw that the cost of doing Friday Fun Day and the monthly newsletter was eating into company profits. Mark made the hard decision to cut both activities down to once a quarter.

Within six months, Mark was informed by HR that the latest engagement survey noted a dramatic drop in job satisfaction. Worse, turnover had increased threefold. Most of the employees who left the company had been hired in those first two years of fast paced growth. Mark was not sure what to do but knew he would have to take quick action if he did not want to jeopardize his ability to serve his current roster of clients.

PinLeader Considerations

- What do you think is going on within this culture?
- What, if anything, should Mark do? Why or why not?
- What would you recommend happen now?
- What should be done in the future?

Quality Matters

Mark has a dilemma. He is trying to do what he believes will help build relationships with employees and clients and remain profitable at the same time. He had attributed the growth of his company to solid customer service and his initial low turnover rate to a family-like atmosphere. Mark has been strong with doing what he believed to be right by the employees and the clients, had a straight plan but pivoted when he needed to and believed himself to be sharp by staying on top of treads. Mark spent time thinking of how to make the company a great place to work. He put significant effort into creating what he believed to be a great company culture.

At some point every business project needs to come together permanently. Like a sewing project with a number of pins in it, the pieces of an organization and its culture need to be sewn together. This juncture, when a culture is sewn together or just pinned together, often marks the point of determination as to whether a culture will thrive or die. Mark was and is an effective leader on the PinLeader Path in many ways. He invests resources into his employees and has established a number of protocols that reaffirm his stated belief of wanting everyone to be treated like family. So what is the problem here?

Simply put, Mark could not sustain what he started. He made the decision to course correct and pivot. But instead of holding to his value of treating employees with value and respect, he made swift changes that impacted his employees with little to no advance warning or explanation. He did not communicate *why* he made the change, failing to be straight-forward with why the pivot has to happen.

What if Mark did not know how to communicate the change? Unlike in times past, where leaders struggled to find the right words to convey a message, Mark had AI as a potential team member to help him with some starter phrases for the communication. Unfortunately, Mark did not utilize the AI platform or consult with anyone on his team. His approach was not strong enough to keep supports in place and the culture began to unravel.

 PinPoint: Sewing is again a good metaphor to illustrate sustainability in your organization. Actions done repeatedly and in a timed rhythm create expectations. Those expectations, in turn, are fulfilled each time the action is done. Ultimately, this builds trust and results in a culture that holds together.

Tradition and Change

Traditions are an example of repeatable actions that contribute to a sustainable work environment. Traditions should be regarded as a binding commitment for a PinLeader. The old saying "Never start something you cannot finish" holds true here. Consistency is essential. Trust is garnered not by words but by consistent action.

Leaders can say that they are just, ethical, and caring; however, if their nonverbal communication demonstrates the opposite then the nonverbal wins and is used as evidence of the opposite every time. As shown in the *PinLeader Respect and Trust Zone* graphic in Chapter 2, the more actions taken and the more external reinforced affirmations build, the more trust is strengthened. Leaders who create cultures that have embedded behaviors and traditions will survive and even thrive when and if they communicate why they are doing what they are doing.

But what about when change is truly needed? In the case of Mark, he had to make changes across the company in order to protect profitability and ensure the company's viability. His initial desire to create traditions to support his employees were on point, but he made changes to these activities without communicating why he was making those changes. Cultures survive and thrive when communication is strong with a clear purpose and outcomes.

Consider a time when a change occurred in your organization that may have negatively impacted a perk of working for the organization. Was the perk eliminated without communication or was it thoughtfully explained? Perhaps it just disappeared as an option. Or it may have been explained but the explanation seemed "weak" or just an excuse for the company not to follow through on its promises. No matter which may have been the case, the result is the same.

Trust begins to erode. Suspicion sets in. Rumors take hold.

> **PinPoint:** If you are not using the right kind of thread in your messaging and communication, your project will unravel. It will not hold. PinLeaders plan carefully when implementing any culture-impacting change. They carefully consider the messaging that will accompany any needed change.

Communicating Change

With clear and compelling messaging, there will always be critics. There will be some who will not believe anything a leader conveys. In every culture there will be naysayers. Energy expended focusing on these individuals and groups is not energy well spent. This is not where leaders should invest their time. Should leaders address concerns and listen to opposing opinions? Of course.

Leaders on the PinLeader Path are strong and effective listeners. These leaders become sharper by allowing differing voices to come through. However, the difference between simply managing a situation and leading a situation is a substantial one.

PinPoint: Leaders have the ability to listen to all sides of a discussion and seek out ways to be inclusive. Ultimately the final decision for implementing change will come down to the leader, but such a process can restore trust and prevent mass departures.

PinLeaders motivate and inspire. In Mark's situation, he had a thriving culture; however, once he made changes that eroded his philosophy for the company with no communication about why the change was being instituted, the culture slowly changed. Since it is the employees who were there in the very beginning who began to leave their positions, the employees had a significant influence on their peers. This was because these long-term employees had earned higher levels of credibility than those with less seniority.

The best solution in a situation is to attempt to bring some of the naysayers to the table. Invite them to help create an ideal solution. If Mark had reached out to employees who shared their frustration with the changes and clearly explained the reasons why he had to make the change, he could have asked his team members to help to come up with creative solutions. Had he involved his employees in a way that encouraged them to share their perspectives and suggestions, it is possible these employees would not have left the company. These very employees might even have been the ones to help craft messaging for others within the organization who were watching the changes and not sure what was going on within the organization.

PinPoint: Offer any team member with a negative attitude toward change an opportunity to be part of the solution. Sometimes team members who feel left out or are never asked their opinions about a change feel they are not part of the fabric and, as a result of their feelings of being rejected, rail against that change.

Pin-Ability

Cultures with leaders who fail to communicate, who make little attempt to address the negative elements, and who do not plan will find the culture will not be effective. Leaders who follow a PinLeader approach understand the dynamics of change. They anticipate how the change might be viewed and misunderstood. This is the leader's *pin-ability*. These leaders are empathic and listen to the needs of their teams, they use resources such as AI when struggling with messaging, and they focus on the needs of the clients.

The goal for any leader should be to create a culture that is sustainable, where employees feel valued and respected and can expect clear communication. PinLeaders who create actions that fulfill their commitments to their team and who meet expectations on a continual basis will enjoy the resulting experience of an organizational culture defined by relationships that are built on trust that is earned. This commitment to creating and continuing to invest in a quality culture leads to sustained growth, even in cases where difficult changes must be made.

Quality Inspection

Have you ever worked on a project and felt relief when the project was over? Was the project so challenging that you second guessed your work and constantly questioned whether you got it right? Did you ever turn to another set of eyes to review your work or gather new perspectives, to check your own thoughts and assumptions, or to catch a potential mistake? Quality control is an important consideration for the PinLeader, and it can prevent embarrassing errors as well as costly mistakes.

Checking Our Work

In the example that opened this chapter, Mark did not have anyone to check his work. Mark did not utilize the resources available to him, such as his team members or AI, to help him with suggestions on wordsmithing his message, primarily because he was not aware of the full extent of the shifting workplace perception among his employees. Instead, he relied on an annual engagement survey to help him decide if employees were satisfied with their work for the company.

At first, Mark appeared to be managing the fast pace of growth well, but as the company's growth continued he began to miss some of the gaps. Those leaders on the PinLeader Path who effectively move organizations forward will not rush the completion of a project or their company's growth. PinLeaders have a straightforward pathway as well as an agreed upon and understood timeline. Leaders are also strong enough in their own character to not deem a project or business move "complete" without taking a second look.

When any project comes to the end of the creation phase, a thorough review is imperative to pause and enlist help to check for any gaps or oversights. Those gaps typically come in two varieties—the superficial and the foundational. Before the evaluation phase begins, the evaluator or group of evaluators must clearly understand the purpose of the project. Once that understanding is firmly in place, the evaluator or evaluation team should be tasked with three chief aims:

1. to determine whether the project goals match the needs,
2. to determine whether actions correspond with the goals, and
3. to determine whether the outcomes match expectations outlined at the outset of the project.

Enlist the Help of Evaluators

Engaging others, including technology, in a review of your work will help you to determine more easily to what degree a gap exists. Once a gap is identified, the next step is to understand the type of gap that may hinder success or cause the project to fail. The first type of gap is the superficial gap. Such gaps are typically able to be addressed with just a few minor changes to a project plan. The gap takes little to no resources.

Even if a superficial gap goes undetected in the early stages of the project, that gap can typically be addressed later in such a way that will not require the PinLeader or others implementing the plan to deviate from stated goals. The second type of gap, the foundational gap, is a much more serious situation.

Any leader who can identify these types of gaps early in the process will fare well. If gaps are not caught early in the process, modifications will still need to be made. In our example, Mark has a problem that goes beyond the superficial. Both his engagement survey results and employee retention have dropped off significantly. Lower scores in the area of retention demonstrate a gap that must be addressed immediately in order to prevent further damage. Although Mark cannot fix the gap for those who have already left the company, there may be an opportunity to restore trust with employees who have stayed.

Another difference between superficial and foundational gaps is that the foundational gap cannot be fixed "down the road." Mark is at a crossroads with his company. The gap in his project is teetering on the edge of becoming a serious foundational gap rather than a superficial gap that can be more easily remedied. The potential need to start over from the beginning when a foundational gap is identified will reap dividends in the end.

As one example, inaccurate project forecasts may lead to out of balance budget allocations which in turn result in longer completion timelines. Foundational gaps require one building block to be placed on top of another in order of importance. The sooner a foundational gap is identified and steps are taken to correct the project plan, the better results a leader can expect. The step by step process is a demonstration of the PinLeader Path, allowing for a straightforward plan and a pivot when the circumstances demand the change.

Address the Gap

In Mark's situation, he created a foundational expectation of having specific benefits and perks for employees who were a part of his team. He may need to go back and adjust his plan to allow for some of those same benefits to continue. Mark can even input the benefits in an AI system.

He can ask if his selected benefits might cause long term challenges or inquire about which benefit choices he may want to consider. Or he might consider offering something that the employees see as even important to replace these initial perks. Either way, Mark must take action to correct the gap identified. If he does not, the repercussions could unravel the company culture he has been devoted to creating for decades and has worked so hard to build.

Even with a careful review of the process, the gaps may not appear right away. Mark created employee benefits as he went along with little to no planning. He needed the time and space to consider the project from different angles, even after he thought he had a solid plan in place. Such evaluation periods may reveal holes that could create even bigger gaps if left unaddressed.

By reviewing what he was doing and checking on trends and other possibilities, Mark would have remained sharp. Here, the saying "sleep on it" or "let it steep" is wisdom for the leader. If others are reviewing a project from their own perspective, providing ample time for that review may help those evaluating a project or plan to catch potential problems sooner rather than later.

Another way that Mark would have been sharper is if he had asked the HR director to help restructure the benefits package. Perhaps a different outcome would have resulted. Leaders who are dedicated to staying on the PinLeader Path recognize when he may be too close to the project. These leaders therefore place a high importance on recruiting to help ensure they have the most objective view and the ability spot potential pitfalls well in advance.

When it comes to leadership, clear and decisive action is important. However, when implementing change, it is essential to build in time for a critical review of project plans and to take the time to carefully consider and thoroughly address potential gaps.

 PinPoint: Look for the holes. Leaders welcome the opportunity to find a gap, knowing that this will save them time and efforts. Address the holes to save the project.

Fixing a Foundational Gap

Depending on where a gap lies in the overall project timeframe, a leader may find the entire project is in question. With foundational gaps in particular, it is important to be prepared and willing to face the fact that sometimes he has to tear out and rework the entire project plan. This "tearing out" does not come lightly and makes the foundational gap the hardest for any leader to address.

A leader will recognize patterns that indicate a plan is wrong for the organization as it does not meet the goals aligned with the mission. The lack of meeting the goals of the organization should be considered a foundational gap. No matter the "wins," noted triumphs, or all the work invested to date toward that plan, the plan is, fundamentally, a failure. In our example, Mark could gain all the accolades from clients and external communities possible, but if he loses his workforce his company will have major problems and may well fold.

Let's look at another example of a foundational gap. Consider a university that has obtained an outside grant and raised money from its alumni and the general community to build a new building for one of its colleges. This appears to be a win. The money has been raised and this could be looked at as a completed project. However, if enrollment for the university has steadily decreased over a number of years to the point the university does not have enough students to fill the classrooms in the new building, the project has a gap.

A leader on the PinLeader Path does not seek out wins to bolster his or her image. Rather, a PinLeader understands the purpose of an organization, in this case to educate students, and keeps the focus on the main goal, in this case recruitment and the retention of existing students. The institution is focused on a singular mission: to support students as they pursue their educational goals, earn a degree and graduate, and successfully pursue their career aspirations. When a leader shifts too much of the attention to the project and ignores the primary goals associated with the organization's mission, gaps will occur.

PinPoint: Tear out and rework. If a leader ignores the gap which may be rooted in a foundational misstep, whatever actions build upon that hole will be misaligned. PinLeaders address gaps even if these gaps are created by their own plans.

The Courage to Lead

The acknowledgement of any gap, whether foundational or superficial, calls on the courage of the leader. Only leaders who have the strength of character to do what is best for the organization will be successful and able to communicate the rationale for their project effectively. PinLeaders bring strength of character, something which will be essential throughout any needed course correction.

What are some of the perceptions that may arise when leaders do seek to address a gap? If leaders utilize an AI interface to find potential gaps, this may be seen as a crutch, similar to utilizing an automated spell check program. Leaders utilizing AI should treat it like any human resource, fully utilizing its knowledge and skill but recognizing its potential flaws. If leaders have a tender ego or are concerned about holding onto power, there is less motivation to correct the gap and therefore a higher likelihood of failure.

Leaders motivated by power over service will focus attention on what they can do well and not tend to the gap. They may redirect problems due to their incompetence and place blame on others. Such leaders usually rely heavily on relationships and shift responsibility to others in order to hold their positions.

PinLeaders, to the contrary will do what is necessary, sometimes with the help of outside evaluation, recognize gaps in project plans. If they do not have the skills to address the gaps on their own, they obtain assistance from other PinLeaders who specialize in those areas. However, if PinLeaders hold positions with titles, such as president or executive director—and especially if they are in such a position for the first time—they should seek out coaches or strong professional development pathways to assist them. In our example, Mark recognized the gaps but he caught them too late; the negative impact of the changes he made without a clear rationale have already begun.

PinPoint: Not everyone is going to embrace or appreciate decisions made by leaders. The PinLeader Path addresses any holes, with or without the support of everyone on the team or across the organization. Leadership is not a popularity contest.

Precision and Popularity

Another consideration that may surround the identified gap is the popularity or lack thereof regarding decisions that must be made around closing a gap. If the leader did not uncover the gap themselves and someone else points the gap out, the PinLeader does not feel threatened. Instead, effective leaders see uncovering the gap as a positive opportunity. They welcome the advisement of others and do not take suggested course corrections personally.

The decisions made around these gaps may not be popular with some inside the organization. Nevertheless, the PinLeader Path demands precision of the PinLeader, and this includes placing the right decision over popular opinion. In the case of Mark, he is not making popular decisions. This is evident from the results of the engagement survey which reveal decreasing satisfaction among employees. He is doing what he feels will save the company and protect its bottom line.

However, Mark has failed to communicate this message to his team. Mark becomes a slightly bent pin because he does not take the information he has and make the necessary changes. Leaders in situations similar to Mark's still need to address the gap and push through to keep projects on track. Doing what is best for the organization is the primary goal, popular or not.

Style it Well

There is a fine line between bragging about success and acknowledging a job well done. There are those leaders who would argue that it is bad form to toot one's own horn. They might say that the best course of action is to let someone else do it for you. These perceptions extend even further. Some within the organization may cast a shadow over a change they do not like. They may also question whether leaders are *good* leaders if these leaders talk too often about their "wins." How do leaders who follow the PinLeader Path own their success without losing credibility?

Wearing Our Success

Mark did not set out to draw attention to himself or the company. He joined the Chamber of Commerce, and the Chamber recognized him for his dedication and business success. While Mark has frequently been asked to share his success story through speaking engagements, he is not actively pursuing accolades.

In an opposite example, we all have been exposed to individuals who went on and on about their achievements, not for the good of the conversation but to boost their own ego. Perhaps you even felt like you needed to escape the conversation. Talking with anyone who will not stop talking about themselves is draining. It can be vampiric in nature and can end up being a one-sided conversation focused only on the person speaking.

It is possible to have this conversation about success in an effective, enriching way but it takes practice. PinLeaders know how to balance messages about their own success using two key pieces of information. First, they have the ability to know and understand the benefit of sharing the information not only for themselves but for the listener. Secondly, they have the ability to *communicate* the message.

PinLeaders deliver the message in such a way that is welcomed by the recipients. They incorporate active listening and allow recipients to share their thoughts in turn. Accomplishing this balance is no simple task. It takes skill to wear success and to wear it well. This came easier for Mark as those external to his company had already invited him to share his achievements.

 PinPoint: Success looks good and is always in fashion. What is not in good taste is talking about others who are failing or incessantly praising your own efforts.

Sharing the Success

Think of a time when you heard a report from a leader about how well his project was going. Did he report only his success? Or did he also share his challenges and problems? Did he speak to how others may have failed before he took over the leadership spot? Or did he celebrate his team and note how the team helped the project succeed?

In each instance a choice was made by the leader in terms of how to convey his success. A leader on the PinLeader Path looks for ways to include his teams. He shares the success. When telling the story of his wins, he cites the benefit of having leaders before him who paved the way for his success. He celebrates his team. A PinLeader does not criticize predecessors who attempted to implement change but failed. Nor does he take sole credit for his own success.

Acknowledging Shortcomings

There is much to be gained from owning wins and successes, but there is also benefit to be gained from acknowledging losses and failures. New opportunities are born from acknowledging the losses and failures. Leaders who demonstrate their sharpness listen to stories that acknowledge shortcomings. They gain leadership wisdom from hearing about where pitfalls and problems may lie along the path to success.

Leaders who openly share about their path to success and problems encountered along the way gives a valuable gift to the listener. PinLeaders are confident and provide information willingly and in a way that uplifts the entire organization or community. They give credit freely and are gracious in their success. In return, they receive what money cannot buy: credibility and admiration, trust and loyalty.

 PinPoint: Leaders convey both successes and challenges, knowing their sharing provides a roadmap for others. They know the listener can benefit for their experience. This authentic sharing *is* success.

Acknowledging Contribution

In the final part of sharing their pathway to success, leaders on the PinLeader Path acknowledge the contribution of others. This acknowledgement of contribution goes beyond just saying it or including their immediate team. PinLeaders readily share the contributions of other leaders who brought their teams together to advance a particular project or the organization as a whole. The decision to include all contributions eventually leads to other leaders sharing their success in a way that honors the contributions of other leaders.

Patterns that work are typically shared with others. This sharing of effective plans is true of the strategic planning process and in most organizations. However, when flaws become apparent in a pattern or a plan, the flaws must be addressed and not duplicated. For example, Mark gave his VP of Operations the opportunity to lead and relied upon his HR director to manage the onboarding process. The challenge is that what Mark put in place was not sustainable when paired with the rapid growth and expansion his company was experiencing.

Mark's leaders may not have been sharp enough to know how to handle the changes and may not have understood what Mark's plan was. However, Mark is sharp enough to eventually be willing to course correct. He may be delayed with listening to the feedback coming from various areas across the organization but is willing to factor in all the information as he determines next steps.

Pin for the Win

A goal for any leader is to know and understand what success is, to share the positive outcomes realized by achieving those successes, and to acknowledge the leaders and team members who helped achieve those successes. This is the golden thread of opportunity that allows the PinLeader to build a culture that can be sustained after various pins are pulled out.

The wise leader prioritizes strategic planning and the careful documentation of the planning process. An emphasis on ongoing dialogue and discussion related to culture building is an important aspect of maintaining culture, and the savvy PinLeader will master the art of storytelling to convey the organization's wins and successes.

So, let's return to Mark's situation. Did he win back the hearts of his employees and save his clients? Was he able to gain back that positive work culture he started with? Since Mark did not plan appropriately before implementing change and failed to communicate the reason why he pulled back and discontinued some of the perks which employees had come to expect, some of the employees who remained with the company began to mention the changes to clients.

When one major client heard the news, they called Mark and offered to underwrite some of the costs associated with the employee programs. Other clients donated food for the employee gatherings. This infused a boost of confidence and lifted morale for the employees. To Mark's surprise, he found employees came to his defense and remained loyal. Mark utilized the engagement surveys to glean suggestions for ways to better support his employees. Again to his surprise, he found many of these suggestions did not have significant costs and were simple to implement.

This PinLeader's *win-ability* was in his *pin-ability*. The answers to his dilemma were found in those surveys. Solutions came through an intimate understanding of his clients. He just needed to listen and learn. Mark later sold his company but negotiated a contract that ensured current employees would maintain their current roles in the new company. His employees were sad to see him leave but were glad for the new connections. Nearly 25 years later, some of those employees still stay in touch with one another, proving that the culture built was true to that family atmosphere.

In organizations that exhibit a strong culture, leaders are present and attuned to the needs and desires of their employees. How leaders decide to lead makes a difference not only to their own success but also to the ultimate success of the organizations they lead. Choosing to develop and maintain a PinLeader Path takes intentional pursuit and a willingness to stay sharp, strong, and straightforward on the path to success.

This PinLeader Path requires leaders to have a strong sense of self awareness and to know who is holding the pin. It necessitates that a leader understand which PinLeader profile they are demonstrating and take the time to learn about the cultures they are stepping into and how they hope to shape the culture. In the final stage, the PinLeader needs to understand why some cultures thrive and others die.

Effective leaders ask for assistance and allow others to review their work. PinLeaders include both human and artificial intelligence in their process and ultimately make them a part of their team. There is no quick path to success. Anyone stating that an organization was an overnight success does not know all that occurred to move the organization where it is today. Only those who have the lived experience and those who have embodied the PinLeader Path will know the struggles faced and recognize the work it took to arrive at that success. Strength of character, sharpness of mind, and the ability to stay straight on path with a pivot when needed will lead to sustainable success.

Ultimately, know that taking the PinLeader Path will lead to greater achievement when successes and failures are shared. PinLeaders are remembered as great leaders because of their effectiveness and willingness to learn from challenging experiences. They remain aware of the contributions of others and dare to lead boldly. Let your leadership story be told by others and be mindful of your teams when you share your story.

Every effective leader has to remain self aware. Every leader must have an intimate understanding of the type of leader she is presently and the type of leader she wants to become. Once this understanding is achieved, it is incumbent upon that leader to intentionally move toward her goal by making the changes necessary to step into her authority and onto the PinLeader Path.

PINLEADER INTERACTIVE

Join the PinLeader Path Community! Scan the QR code below to access the PinLeader Interactive. Use the following questions for further discussion and consideration.

The Case of Threading It All Together

- What are the ways you prefer to communicate as a leader? Why is this your preference?

- What is the hardest message that you have had to communicate? What occurred after you communicated the message?

- What advice would you give to other leaders about communicating messages about change?

- What are some of the best ways you have utilized to communicate successes and wins?

RESOURCES

Mays & Associates, Ltd.

Visit www.maysassociatesltd.com to learn more about working with Dr. Gore and the MAYS team, connect to the PinLeader™ Podcast and find a wealth of resources on our blog.

PinLeader™ Podcast

Pictured: Host Dr. Shanda Gore with Ms. Tisha Mays

PinLeader Blog

PinLeader™: The Perils of Micromanaging and Why Letting Go Can Lead to Greater Success

A PinLeader, an effective leader with desired attributes

Do you know your company's strategic plan?

Benjamin Franklin once said, "By failing to prepare, you are preparing to fail." Preparing for success takes a lot

Managing Difficult Team Members

Leadership is a multifaceted journey filled with triumphs but also challenges. One of the most common hurdles that leaders encounter is...

ACKNOWLEDGEMENTS

My first thank you goes to God and the guiding force to live my life with purpose.

I would not be who I am today without my loving parents, Arthur Mays and Betty Tomlinson Mays, who shaped me and provided my first love of education. A heartfelt thanks goes to my loving husband Bobby and to my now adult children Nathan and Shoshanah who have stood by me and encouraged me. Every day, my family demonstrates to me the power of difference. They show me that there is always so much more to consider.

There are so many to thank concerning the actual application of a PinLeader mindset, but I would be remiss if I did not first acknowledge our Mays and Associates colleagues Ms. Jini Jordan, Ms. Marie Dunn, and Ms. Dianne Engler who have worked alongside me and to the clients who have been part of my experience. Our firm has grown exponentially, and it is because of you that I remain focused to keep up the work. Thank you for your invaluable contributions!

I want to offer a note of appreciation to the 2005 Bowling Green State University Education Leadership Cohort Class and to the colleagues who sat and patiently listened to me first describe the PinLeader concept. In particular I want to thank Dr. Kim Kirkland, who kept asking where my book was. Well, here it is my friend, as promised.

ABOUT THE AUTHOR

Host of the PinLeader Podcast, Dr. Shanda Gore is founder and president of Mays and Associates, Ltd. (MAYS), a full-service leadership development, strategic planning, and culture building consulting firm. With more than two decades of experience in leading organizations for change, Dr. Gore leads the MAYS team of experts that works with organizations from city and county municipalities, private corporations, K-12 systems, public and private universities, and large athletic organizations. She is a highly sought-after executive coach and speaker known for driving lasting and impactful change. Her expertise in guiding leaders and organizations toward success has earned her a reputation for excellence and results.

Dr. Gore has been interviewed by the Big10 Network for her work with the college football officials in the Big Ten, MAC, Missouri Valley, and Pioneer conferences. More than 22,000 individuals have benefitted from her training workshops. Dr. Gore is also a keynote speaker who has led discussion topics at conferences and has conducted workshops on leadership, disparities in health care, strategic planning, organizational change, engagement surveys, and policy implications. Her speaking engagements have included the annual meetings for the Association for American Medical Colleges, the National Conference on Race and Ethnicity, and the Higher Learning Commission.

Dr. Gore is a graduate of Bowling Green State University, where she received a Bachelor's of Communications as well as a Master's of Mass Communication and a Doctor of Education in Leadership Studies. Dr. Gore has been married for thirty years to retired firefighter Bobby Lee Gore, Jr. They are the proud parents of two wonderful grown children, Nathaniel Gore and Shoshanah Gore.